Prisoner of War
Testimonio of Suhasini Biswas

Prisoner of War
Testimonio of Suhasini Biswas

Jayati Gupta

Orient BlackSwan

PRISONER OF WAR: TESTIMONIO OF SUHASINI BISWAS

ORIENT BLACKSWAN PRIVATE LIMITED

Registered Office
3-6-752 Himayatnagar, Hyderabad 500 029, Telangana, India
Email: centraloffice@orientblackswan.com

Other Offices
Bengaluru, Chennai, Guwahati, Hyderabad, Kolkata, Mumbai,
New Delhi, Noida, Patna

© Orient Blackswan Private Limited 2026
First published 2026

ISBN 978 93 6973 337 8

Typeset in Cambria 13/15 *by*
K. Divya, Hyderabad 500 060

Printed at
Manipal Technologies Limited., Manipal

Published by
Orient Blackswan Private Limited
3-6-752, Himayatnagar,
Hyderabad 500 029, Telangana, India
Email: info@orientblackswan.com

The publisher has endeavoured to ensure that the URLs for external websites referred to in this book are correct and active at the time of going to press. However, the publisher has no responsibility for the websites and can make no guarantee that a site will remain live or that the content is or will remain appropriate.

In loving memory of
Sujoy Gupta (1950–2022)
An epitome of gentleness and compassion

Dedicated to all who were victims of trauma
in the Second World War (1939–1945)

Contents

Acknowledgements

Writing this acknowledgement is, for me, an emotionally charged moment. It brings to mind several individuals whose memories are intrinsic to the project. My aunt-in-law, Sreela Sen, is remembered first because she had treasured Suhasini's copy of *Gitanjali*, keeping it in her safe custody before handing it over to me. I am equally grateful to Sudhir Madhab Bose, Suhasini's nephew, who shared the correspondence and the blue exercise-book from her internee days. It was my husband, Sujoy, who felt that 'Nedu Mashi', with whom he had interacted, had been too reticent to speak of her past sufferings. Yet her saga of endurance and hope constitutes an off-beat story of Indian womanhood. Sadly, those to whom I am indebted for the archival sources and reminiscences are no longer there to read the book.

When I seriously thought of researching the subject, the support I received from Roger Mansell, the founder of the Center for Research, Allied POWs Under the Japanese, was encouraging. He not only gave me permission to use material from the website he created and maintained but put me in touch with researchers on the ground. Thank you, Wes Injerd, Yukako Ibuki, and Mayumi Komiya, for your interest in Suhasini. It is unfortunate that Roger Mansell has passed away, and I am unable to connect again with the other researchers, as their emails are not being delivered at the addresses that I have.

My email friendship with Michael Charnaud has been the highlight of this project. He shared his own reminiscences, the diary notes of Alfred Round, and the group photograph taken at the camp in August 1945. He introduced me to

Robert Murphy so that I was able to access his dissertation. I had hoped to share the book with Michael, but that was not destined to be. Luckily, I have recently been able to contact his son Paul Charnaud, who has very kindly shared pictures of the Convent that he visited with his family in 2007.

The person behind my productive visit to the Imperial War Museum, London, was Rod Suddaby, the Keeper of the Department of Documents. I regret that, at that time, though I was allowed to click a few photographs of Round's diary made from slivers of paper and cardboard, I had not applied formally for permission to reproduce it in any publication.

Safe handling of the archival material, which had mostly fading pencilled-in notes, was a major issue every time I used a magnifying glass to read the handwritten texts. Abhijit Gupta, Director, Jadavpur University Press, very kindly stepped in to digitise the archival material at the School of Cultural Texts and Records of the University. I am deeply indebted to him for this timely intervention. Most of the images used alongside the text in this book are from the files digitised, courtesy Abhijit Gupta.

The book is unlikely to have seen the light of day without Padmaja Anant and Sreenath S. believing that the story I wanted to tell had some potential worth. I am happy to have signed the contract with Orient BlackSwan, who assigned me very meticulous editors—Mahalakshmi, who did the copyediting, and Aditi Jha. It has been such a pleasure working with Aditi, who helped me improve the narrative. Often, while trying to get the facts right, the reticent personality of Suhasini kept disappearing. The comments and editing put me back on track to focus on foregrounding the protagonist, a lady of remarkable dignity and moral stamina. Behind any publication is a skilled production team that looks after all the physical nitty-gritties. In consultation with the editor, they have indeed taken a lot of care.

The process of writing and research took much longer than I had intended. There were frustrating breaks—work pressures, health issues, chaotic schedules and irreversible personal losses. Each time, coming back was like another new start, when the finishing line seemed so distant. My family solidly stood by me, reminding me through their patience that I was committed to voicing a truth that had remained untold.

All the images used in this book are from my personal collection, unless otherwise stated. Wherever this is not the case, the relevant image courtesy has been duly acknowledged.

Jayati Gupta

Preface

For by my glee might many men have laughed,
And of my weeping something had been left,
Which must die now. I mean the truth untold.
The pity of war, the pity war distilled.
Wilfred Owen (1893–1918)

It may have been the late 1990s when, through family sources, I heard with great interest and in considerable detail about Suhasini Biswas from Calcutta (now Kolkata), who had survived incarceration as a POW in Japan and had returned to India but never shared her experiences publicly. By then, it had been almost twenty years since Suhasini had passed away and been buried in the family crypt at the Lower Circular Road Cemetery in Kolkata.

After her release and return, Suhasini led a life dedicated to education and social service—a selfless existence. Not much was known or spoken about her having been held for more than three years in a civilian internment camp in Japan during the Second World War, almost lost to the world and to her family. The experience had undoubtedly been deeply traumatic, and these were years she may have wished to erase from her memory. As a result, the physical testimonies of her camp days—the sparse communication from that period, the copy of Rabindranath Tagore's *Gitanjali* that had been her constant companion, and a notebook or two in which she scribbled her thoughts—were tucked away in an obscure corner of her home.

I became interested in Suhasini's life when I first heard the story of her Second World War experiences, narrated by my aunt-in-law, Sreela Sen, who also showed me the copy of

Suhasini's *Gitanjali* that she had rescued. The story of how this particular copy—Suhasini's companion in the POW camp, in which she had written in Bengali her thoughts, details, and observations as she lived through those years—was nearly sold off along with old newspapers and accumulated rubbish to a roadside vendor, is a reminder of our neglect of family history and the low value we often place on memory and remembrance. By sheer chance, the volume was saved when my late aunt-in-law volunteered to retrieve it and keep it with her so she could read the fading pencilled entries that bore witness to momentous historical events. I first set eyes on the tattered book when it was in her safekeeping.

Several years later, my husband Sujoy and I went to meet her nephew, Sudhir Madhab Bose,[1] a longstanding and elderly friend of the family. My purpose was to see whether he could help me build further on the hair-raising story of Suhasini. He brought out a plastic packet containing official communications and telegrams from the shipping company about the interception of the vessel on which Suhasini was returning from Australia to India in April 1942, when she was taken prisoner. He also handed me a set of photocopies of the material in his possession. The packet contained a tattered ruled notebook, a few letters, and picture cards— but not the *Gitanjali*, which had already been rescued earlier.

The original plastic packet, with the shipping company's messages sent from time to time to Suhasini's sister,

---

[1] Sudhir Madhab Bose died in 2002 at the age of ninety. He began his career as a WBCS officer and his honesty and expertise drew the attention of Dr B. C. Roy, the Chief Minister of West Bengal (1948–62). He served as special officer at the Writers' Building during Roy's tenure and subsequent chief ministers. He retired in 1970 as an IAS officer. He was also Secretary and trustee on several committees of the Calcutta Diocese and the Church of Northern India.

Surama Biswas, Inspectress of Schools posted in Dhaka, and last known to be in Sudhir Madhab's custody, became untraceable among family members after his passing. Nor were any original photographs or additional letters, if they existed, accessible. The corpus of archival material, if it may be called that, was minimal.

As I went through the handwritten snippets of information, along with the pencilled entries in the *Gitanjali*—which Vivek Das, a professional photographer then with the *Ananda Bazar* Group, had kindly transferred to a compact disc for easier handling—I wondered how to fill in the many gaps. My aunt-in-law shared some anecdotal memories of Suhasini and spoke of how 'Nedu Mashi' (nicknamed *Nedu*, meaning 'bald' in Bangla, because she had lost her hair and a great deal of weight after her ordeal as a POW) spent several months, after her return, in the Dhaka home of her maternal grandfather, Girish Chandra Nag, and his family, who were close friends of the Biswas family of Calcutta's 4, Mullen Street.

I still needed to uncover much more information about the POW camps in Japan to gain a clearer understanding of the conditions prevailing at the time. I realised that I would have to trace a sequence of events shaped by major political decisions made by the contending Axis and Allied powers. Defining moments such as the attack on Pearl Harbour (7 December 1941), the bombing of Hiroshima (6 August 1945) and Nagasaki (9 August 1945), and the surrender of Japan (14 August 1945), which ended the war, directly affected the internees in the camps.

By the time I began searching for factual details, the World Wide Web was revolutionising access to information. Almost by chance, I came upon an internet site maintained by Roger Mansell,[2] who had extensively researched the

---

[2] http://www.mansell.com/POW_resources/camplists/sendai/fukushima/fukushima.htm

subject. I was excited to find that Suhasini Biswas was listed as one of the British Indian civilian internees at the Fukushima camp in Japan, although her name and gender were recorded incorrectly. I quickly learned how to contact Roger Mansell, and he replied promptly. Thus began an email correspondence from September 2009, not only with Mansell but with on-site researchers such as Wes Injerd, Mayumi Komiya, Yukako Ibuki and Ron Taylor—all of whom were eager to help ensure that these untold stories of personal courage and endurance were shared.

Meanwhile, as I prepared to visit the UK in March 2010, I contacted the Imperial War Museum in Lambeth, London, to enquire whether they held any archival material relating to civilian internees in Japanese camps. Roderick Suddaby, then Keeper of Records, very kindly prepared whatever relevant material the IWM possessed. The items I found there were invaluable, corroborating or explaining the cryptic notes Suhasini had written in an assortment of places. Among them was a manuscript reconstructing the story of the sinking of the *SS Kirkpool*,[3] written by Alfred Calvert Round, an internee at the Fukushima prison camp and dated 21 March 1945 (catalogue number 91/31/1). This handwritten diary begins with events from May 1942, and is inscribed on a small pad made from slivers of paper and cardboard, presumably from boxes supplied in parcels distributed by the International Red Cross. The makeshift pad is stitched at the top and perhaps later stapled.

I learned from Mayumi Komiya's research—based on written accounts of Australian nurses of Rabaul who were in a Japanese POW camp near Yokohama, unknown to the world for three years and nine months—that many diaries

---

[3] In the Nautilus archives (nautilusint.org) a detailed, 14-page document written by the 27-year-old chief officer, Olaf Olsen of the British merchant ship *Kirkpool* is preserved. Only 32 of the crew survived the attack by a German raiding vessel and of these 17 were held in the Fukushima camp.

kept by internees were undated, written in shorthand or private notations, and compiled haphazardly so that the factual details remained encrypted to avoid confiscation by camp authorities. This partly explains why Suhasini's scribbled thoughts appear so scattered: written in one corner of a notebook, in margins, beside a song in the *Gitanjali*,[4] or on its flyleaf, invariably in Bengali, which neither the Japanese nor the transnational internee community could decipher.

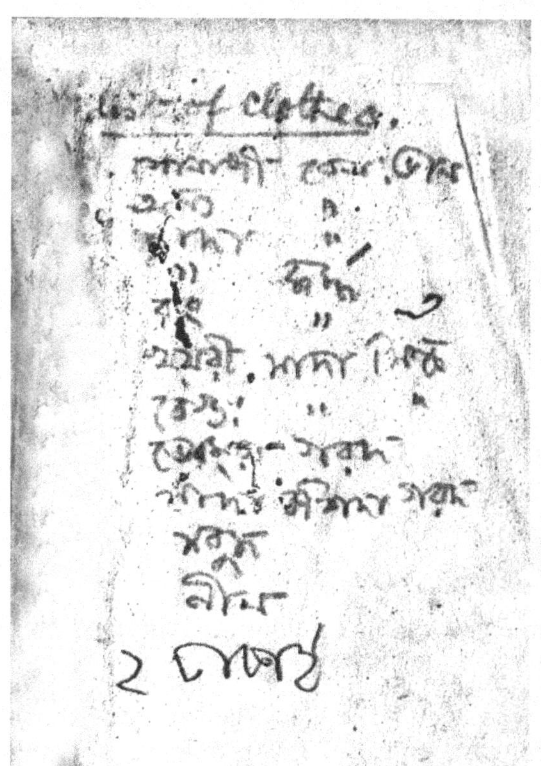

The flyleaf with Suhasini's scribblings

[4] Suhasini had with her the 1925 edition of Tagore's *Gitanjali*. All references in this book are to the 1925 edition unless otherwise specified.

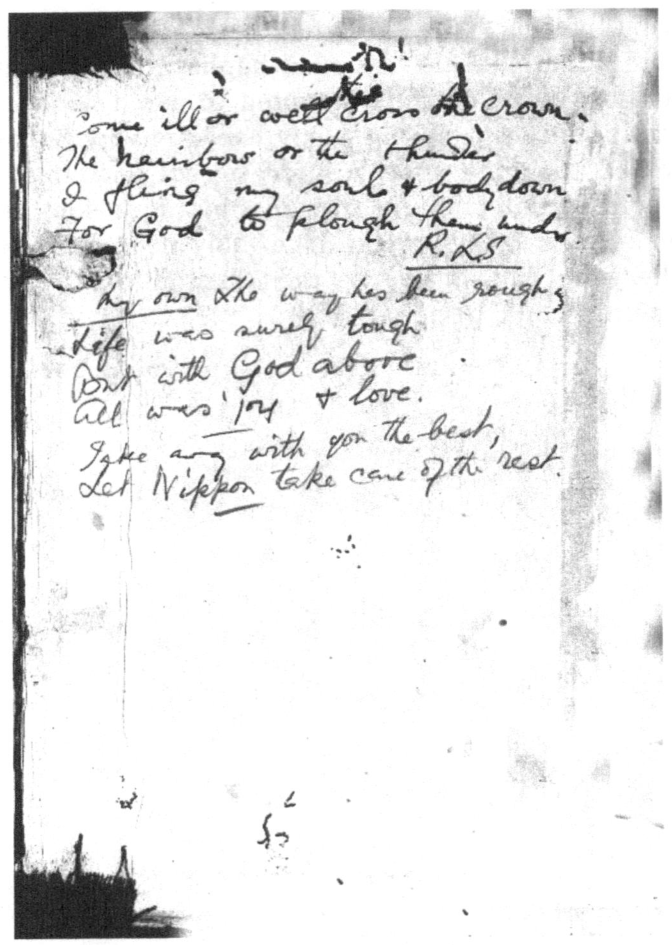

On the last page of Gitanjali *are farewell messages from Suhasini's camp mates*

Suhasini was friendly, easy to get along with, self-effacing and reticent—a private person even as she shared in the travails of the other prisoners, both men and women, and especially the children in the camp. Evidence of her quiet, supportive presence in the community, and of her participation in the spiritual life of the internees, appears in Round's manuscript diary preserved in the Imperial War Museum, as well as in Andy Millar's account based on original documents of his father's experiences as a POW, in the book *Lost at Sea, Found at Fukushima* (2012).

I became even more convinced that this was a unique eyewitness experience that needed to be retrieved and shared. It revealed how one's personal life could be shaped by wartime events and offered insight into how civilian movements were affected by political decisions. Many of the entries provide what may be called a ringside perspective on the Second World War, which dominated the international arena throughout the period of Suhasini's internment until the end of the war, marked by Emperor Hirohito's recorded announcement of Japan's surrender on 14 August 1945.

Despite my desire to bring forth Suhasini's story to the world, I remained apprehensive about the sparse archival material available to me. How could I piece together her story from so little? Suhasini's entries are not conventional diary entries: she had no diary, but instead wrote in margins and empty spaces in the single exercise book that survived, recording incidents with or without dates. It is for this reason that I have used the term *testimonio* in the title to refer to the factual daily events documented in her scribbled notes—a form of witnessing to the collective and shared trauma endured by the internees in the Japanese camp. I do not use the term to imply a sequential first-person narrative.

Even more intriguing is the manner in which Rabindranath Tagore's *Gitanjali*, in the original Bengali, became Suhasini's intimate space for pencilling in some reflective comments, confessions, event records, and articulations of hopes and desires that perhaps seemed to converse directly with the printed text.

The copy of Tagore's 1925 Gitanjali *edition that Suhasini owned*

In the context of the expanding, heterogeneous and interdisciplinary field of memory studies, recovering the past through recollection becomes a complicated task. I found no methodological framework that enabled the use of an unrelated third-person perspective to retrieve memories based on marginalia. The material I was reconstructing emerged from the lived experience of another subject who had endured trauma; it was, therefore, a form of retelling. The imperative question that arose was: what theoretical tools should I employ to recover the immediacy of this material so many decades later? When a subject is self-reflexive and recalls events, recollects memories, and retrieves a past, the narrative falls within the purview of contemporary multidimensional research on human memory. My attempt, however, was to reconstruct an eyewitness account of individual and collective trauma by corroborating evidence from co-prisoners in the Fukushima camp. Moreover, Suhasini's self-musings introduced another dimension, situating herself—as a British Indian subject—within the broader context of the freedom struggle in colonial India, a movement gaining momentum and shaping the destiny of her motherland at a crucial moment in global history.

I have attempted, in this monograph, to narrate Suhasini's story of endurance and courage, which has never ceased to astonish me. Travelling solo, internationally, while the Second World War was escalating in Europe, was a high-risk undertaking. It appears to have been a leap of faith for Suhasini, her family, and Baptist friends who believed deeply that nothing would go amiss under God's protection. Her harrowing time as a POW was equally significant: her inner resilience enabled her to negotiate the challenges of cohabiting in the camp with internees of varied age groups, temperaments, races, backgrounds, and religious leanings. Rational and balanced, she internalised the conflicts she witnessed and sought solace from within. Her cheerful and helpful demeanour carried her through the ordeal. In many ways, she defied the stereotype of an Indian woman (though internee records list her as a British civilian) and emerged not only as educated, but fearless and patriotic. She survived the physical and mental traumas of an extraordinary experience and chose not to foreground her story, leaving it to others to uncover a truth long untold.

1

Experience as History

The Second World War (1939–1945) was a devastating global conflict that was not only about countries and nations at war but, as all wars do, exposed a vast human drama of loss, treachery and betrayal that reshaped the course of history. Its theatres ranged geographically from China, Japan and South Asia in the East, to Europe and Russia in the West, extending across Britain, the Americas, Africa and Australia, and spanning the Atlantic, Pacific and Indian Oceans. As strategic political alliances were forged, polarising the world into the Axis powers and the Allies, ordinary people found themselves caught in existential dilemmas that foregrounded identities and loyalties. This account traces the true-life experience of a Bengali woman who, as a British civilian prisoner of war in Japan, endured extreme violence, uncertainty and isolation—yet remains largely unknown and unsung in Bengal and India, an individual submerged in the tide of momentous global events. Swept into the vortex of history, her transnational experience of endurance and survival stands as one among many heroic narratives of the war. As a woman-survivor of the Great War, her eyewitness testimony reveals the trauma borne by her and other internees—a micro-narrative of suffering and resilience absent from official histories. As a subject of a colonised homeland, she remained withdrawn and reticent, reluctant to consciously record or archive her testimonio, a silence that may, in contemporary psychotherapeutic terms, reflect the effects of stress-related trauma and a form of dissociative amnesia.[1]

In a sense, to retrieve and reconstruct Suhasini's experience from the cryptic notes, desultory pencilled-in entries, diary-like marginalia, letters, and the few surviving records of her months in captivity is to create what Romila Thapar calls 'a kind of *pointillist* history—rather like the style of painting—a collection of unconnected dots which taken together compose a picture' (2000, 3). Yet, even these 'dots' must be carefully contextualised, for the fragments being pieced together were embedded in a specific historical time and location; the larger picture can only emerge when such individual experiences are woven into the broader tapestry of global history. A testimonio does not fit into a linear historical pattern. Rather, it opens up alternative perspectives that help explore and recover historical memory. The term 'testimonio'—as used in literary and culture studies—originates from Latin American/Hispanic sources.

> This type of writing entails a first person oral or written account, drawing on experiential, self-conscious, narrative practice to articulate an urgent voicing of something to which one bears witness. Presented at times as memoirs, oral histories, qualitative vignettes, prose, song lyrics, or spoken word, the testimonio has the unique characteristic of being a political and conscienticized reflection that is often spoken. (Reyes and Rodriguez 2012, 525)

---

[1] Dissociative amnesia is a form of mind-block when a person tries to distance oneself from traumatic experiences. It creates gaps in one's memories to protect oneself from remembering distressing events.

This particular testimonio is structured as a third-person narrative retelling; however, since it is reconstructed from the protagonist's experiential notes, it can perhaps be regarded as the testimonio of an experience situated within a unique context of a larger and more globalised political history. This becomes significantly complicated when the identity of the protagonist is positioned within the paradox of being both a subject of an imperial and colonised nation and a British civilian. The trajectory of Suhasini's life intersects with India's nationalist history as it unfolded during these years. If a basic feature of any testimonio is that it 'allows the narrator to show an experience that is not only liberating in the process of telling but also political in its production of awareness to listeners and readers alike' (ibid., 527), then exploring Suhasini's scribblings can, even after so many decades, offer insight into a crucial phase in the education and empowerment of women in India.

In the later decades of the nineteenth century and the early years of the twentieth, the lives of a section of Indian women were being transformed through access to education and increased participation in the public sphere. This sociohistorical backdrop frames the exceptional events of Suhasini's life.

Suhasini Biswas was born on 31 December 1895 into a Bengali Christian family living in what is today South Calcutta—then situated on the extreme periphery of the white town and far removed from the traditional zamindari and upper-class native households of the northern parts of the city. The family home at 4 Mullen Street still stands. It was here that she was born, it became the refuge to which she returned after her horrific experiences in the Japanese civilian internee camp, and it remained her home until her death on 28 December 1970.

Hiralal and Sarat Kumari Biswas had a large family of seven children—five girls and two boys. Suhasini's childhood would have been typical of a young girl in a 'native Christian' household, markedly different from an upbringing within a conservative or orthodox Hindu family. Education, regular church-going, and the inculcation of strong moral values and self-reliance were central aspects of this Christian background—principles that would later sustain her morally through the traumatic years of captivity.

Within walking distance of the family home stood one of the oldest missionary high schools for girls in South Calcutta. Established first as the Diocesan Mission School in 1876 by Ms. Angelina Margaret Hoare, a missionary from Kent, along with Miss Milman from England, the institution gained recognition for its role in advancing girls' education. After Ms. Hoare's death in 1892, Bishop Johnson of Calcutta ensured the continuation of her work, and in 1894— just a year before Suhasini's birth—the school was entrusted to the Clewer Sisters (later known as the Sisters of Mercy) of the Convent of St. John the Baptist and renamed St. John's Diocesan School. It received official recognition by the Bengal Government in 1900, and in time a women's college was established in the same compound. It was therefore only natural that Suhasini completed her schooling, undergraduate degree, and teachers' training at this institution.

Few details survive regarding Suhasini's early life beyond these basic facts. After completing her training, she travelled to Allahabad (now Prayagraj) to take up a job at Jagat Taran Girls' High School (now known as Jagat Taran Golden Jubilee School). Although the exact duration of her tenure is unknown, she became the Principal of the school, which was a pioneering institution in promoting women's emancipation through education. By the early decades of the twentieth century, women's education in India had already gained a strong foothold. The work of Christian missionaries and their *zenana* education initiatives, the liberal ideas of the Brahmo Samaj, the reformist efforts of Raja Rammohan Roy and Pandit Ishwar Chandra Vidyasagar, and the transformative ideals of the Arya Samaj together created an intellectual and social climate conducive to progressive policies and significant advances in the sphere of women's education.

Very significantly, Suhasini may be seen as someone nurtured by the social reform movements of nineteenth-century India, which intersected with the growing nationalist movement, helping women enter public life as teachers and social workers. The promotion of women's education was central to efforts aimed at transforming their status, emancipating them, and restoring rights long denied under traditional patriarchal systems. It must be noted, however, that the women being referred to here—and Suhasini in particular—belonged to a progressive, urban, and relatively exclusive social milieu in which the roles of women were already being redefined.

Both social reformers and liberal activists viewed women's education as a crucial means of improving their social standing and enabling genuine empowerment. Even cultural revivalists, who regarded women as preservers of tradition and stabilising forces within the family, supported female education as a way to protect and reinforce values that could resist indiscriminate Westernisation and conversion. While reformists and liberals continued to imagine women's roles primarily within the domestic sphere, the possibility of those boundaries being transgressed—and women assuming more visible roles in the public domain—became increasingly tangible.

Suhasini, like her elder sister Surama, dedicated her life to women's education, pursuing it as both a profession and a personal mission. After her tenure at Jagat Taran Girls' High School in Allahabad, she went on to teach and later head the Faizunnesa High School for Girls[2] in Comilla (Kumilla, then part of undivided Bengal and now in Bangladesh), which in the late 1920s and 1930s was a vibrant district town of the sprawling Bengal Presidency. Her appointment to the prestigious Provincial Education Service in Bengal was a significant achievement, as it meant that she could be posted anywhere within the Presidency, which included Assam, Odisha, and Bihar. The *Calcutta Gazette* of 3 November 1932 carried the notification: 'Miss Suhasini Biswas, officiating Headmistress, Faizunessa High School for Girls, Comilla, will continue to act in the appointment and in the Bengal Educational Service (Women's Branch), vice Mrs. Bidhubala Bakshi, transferred.'[3] This marked her formal entry into the Bengal Provincial Service.

Suhasini's career thus, countered dominant perceptions of Indian womanhood and exemplified the beginnings of social change that had taken root in early twentieth-century India. She represented the emerging figure of the 'new woman' who stepped beyond the traditional trajectory of marriage, childbirth and domesticity to promote a progressive vision of womanhood—one that imagined women as educated, informed, independent-minded individuals prepared to participate in the salient debates of the time. Suhasini herself was deeply committed to a

---

[2] What is now Nawab Faizunnesa Government Girls' High School was established in 1873 by Faizunnesa Chaudhurani, a zamindar who realised the need for setting up an educational institution for Muslim girls practising purdah. Interestingly the medium of instruction was Bengali (rather than Urdu or Persian) though the students were also taught English. It was upgraded to a high school in 1931. Unfortunately, no pre-Independence records of the school are available.

[3] Calcutta Gazette, November 3, 1932, Part I-B. Notification: Tippera- No. 3073 T. Edn.—25 October 1932.

professional career and to the social and moral upliftment of women.

Her mobility is a case in point. Early in her career she chose to live away from home—first in Allahabad and later in Comilla. It was in Comilla that she came into close contact with Australian Baptist missionaries,[4] whose presence and activities in regions such as Comilla, Sirajganj, Faridpur, Mymensingh, Noakhali and Sylhet had been prominent since the 1880s. The mission fields[5] designated for Australian women missionaries, as well as the range of responsibilities entrusted to them in India, were far broader and more demanding than what they might have been permitted in their own country. Many adventurous Australian women took up roles as preachers, teachers, nurses and doctors, devoting themselves to missionary work that was often framed as part of the larger 'evangelising mission'—what the British in India rationalised as the 'White Wo/Man's Burden', a supposedly civilising mission directed at the 'heathen natives'.

Suhasini was deeply influenced by the work and presence of these Australian women missionaries in Comilla and, as a Christian herself, became close to several of them. Among the enduring friendships she formed was her association with Edna Hale, who visited churches in the district as a delegate of the Australian Baptist Foreign Mission.

---

[4] Ellen Arnold (1858–1931), a South Australian teacher, was a pioneering Baptist missionary. She bought land in Comilla and started building the Mission House in 1889 and moved there in 1890. The Australian Baptist Foreign Mission Society had a regular presence in Faridpur, Comilla and Pubna.

[5] Missions and missionary work in different regions—India, Australia or other parts of Asia or Africa.

The flier advertising Hale's visit

Suhasini's intrepid decision to travel to Australia, and the itinerary she followed—likely including Fremantle, Adelaide, Melbourne, Sydney and Brisbane—was largely orchestrated and facilitated by her circle of Baptist missionary friends. A few days after she had sailed from the shores of India, her mother wrote to her in Bengali in a letter dated 12 November 1941:

I am penning a few lines to you, knowing how happy you would be to see my handwriting. Ever since you left we are feeling very sad; all the time, you were so helpful to everyone, lending a hand in every household chore. We are missing you as we were so used to you always bustling up and down the stairs and being all about the home. It is already ten days now, but there is no chance of getting any news. I hope you are well and rested and are enjoying the sea-breeze. Did you experience sea-sickness?[5]

Suhasini's mother's letter

---

[6] The letter is hand-written in Bengali. It underlines the fact that Suhasini belonged to a family where women of the previous generation were also exposed to education.

These words of love and concern were interspersed with gentle exhortations not to worry about her siblings or her mother, as '*by God's grace, everything will be fine*'. She wished her daughter a safe journey and urged her to remain calm and mentally at ease. There is a strong conviction in the letter that the friends accompanying Suhasini who were very fond of her would look after her with care. The journey is described as a rare opportunity not granted to many, an instance of divine blessing and grace. She closes with the prayer, '*May the Lord protect you from danger*'. The letter is permeated throughout with absolute and unwavering faith in God.

Suhasini's visit to Australia came just about a month before the surprise military attack by the Imperial Japanese Navy and Air Force on Pearl Harbour on the morning of 7 December 1941—an event that would dramatically alter the course of the Second World War. The US naval base in Hawaii was severely damaged, and the next day the United States entered the Pacific War by declaring hostilities against Japan. Although undertaking a sea voyage during wartime was undoubtedly risky, the rapid escalation of conflict in the Pacific could not have been foreseen.

With the war shifting towards the Pacific, Australia—until then somewhat distant from the battles raging across Europe—found itself suddenly vulnerable. Earlier that year, with conditions in war-torn Europe deteriorating, Madeline Charnaud had travelled to Australia with her ten-year-old son, Michael, seeking safety. But once the United States retaliated after Pearl Harbour, the geopolitical landscape changed rapidly, turning the Pacific into an active theatre of war and forcing many, including the Charnauds, to leave the island nation.

A year later, Madeline made the decision to return to Colombo, where her husband was working as a tea planter. Meanwhile, Suhasini's sojourn in Australia was also drawing to a close and her return to India became imminent. By coincidence, Michael Charnaud and his mother sailed out of Melbourne on the same ship as Suhasini. The ten-year-old would later recall the profound insecurity and uncertainty of those days in his memoir:[7]

> ...everyone had a feeling of foreboding as Australia seemed so huge and vulnerable with most of its small army in the Middle East defending the Suez Canal. Over the next few weeks the Japanese made a lightning attack through Malaya followed by the surrender of Britain's Great Far Eastern Naval Base of Singapore. The Dutch East Indies were quickly overrun and shortly after that Darwin was savagely bombed and everyone expected the Japanese to land in Australia at any moment.

Notwithstanding this atmosphere of anxiety and fear, Suhasini took the opportunity to travel within Australia, primarily visiting Baptist missions and spending time with friends who offered her hospitality and care. She did not keep an archive of her experiences, nor have any letters she may have written home, survived. However, a number of letters addressed to her remain, in which her friends fondly remembered 'Bishy's' visit to their homes, to their church, and to the Easter service when '...*everyone here (Ashfield, New South Wales) had fallen in love with you...*'.[8]

One such letter was from H. G. Redman of 4A Ningana Avenue, King's Park, Adelaide—father of her Baptist friend Jess. Jess had been in India and spent time with Suhasini's sister Surama, and according to Redman's letter dated 29 September 1945, she had given the family '*much information from her diary of your movements in Adelaide and Melbourne*' before that fated voyage home on the

------

[7] http://www.bbc.co.uk/history/ww2peopleswar/stories/79/a4220579.shtml

[8] This is from a letter dated 24/8/1945, after the prisoners were released, written by Helen O. Cousin, of Ashfield, New South Wales, Australia, to Miss Biswas as 'a welcome note to await you in India, home!'

Nankin. Redman fondly recollects Suhasini's time in Adelaide, her wardrobe of 'nice saris', and the warmth and companionship of her stay in their home.

Suhasini's calm demeanour, her ability to connect with people, and her genuine concern for others endeared her to acquaintances and friends alike, and undoubtedly helped her endure the unexpected hardship that lay ahead. It was on her return journey in April–May 1942 that she was suddenly drawn into the vortex of the widening Second World War. Unaware of the traumatic events about to unfold, Edna Hale wrote to her on 17 April 1942:

> Hope you have the best of trips and have much joy on your return to the homeland... It was hard to see you go and not be able to accompany you. I know, however, you are in good hands and shall not worry on that score. And if all goes well I shall join you before the end of the year. Please send me a cable as soon as you arrive and I shall be able to inform the others.

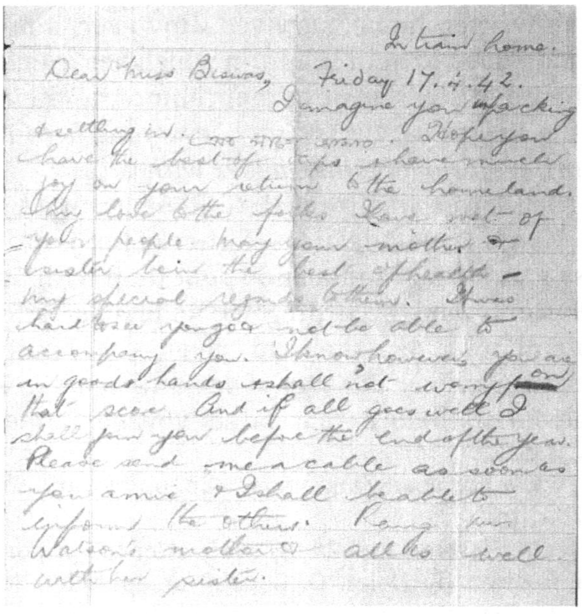

Edna Hale's letter of April 1942 to Suhasini

2

Trapped By Events

In an era when instant communication is taken for granted, the posted hand-written letter, wireless telegram, or cablegram now appear obsolete. During the First and Second World Wars, the volatile interwar years, and for several years thereafter, these modes of communication were considered the only lifelines connecting families, friends, and communities across continents. Military departments, too, relied on cablegrams for urgent dispatches, as they were deemed more secure than letters, which could be easily intercepted.

Receiving a cablegram in wartime was invariably fraught with anxiety and dread. Given the strict limitations on word count, cables were terse and often chilling in tone, composed with an economy of words that nonetheless conveyed grave urgency.

On 26 May 1942, Suhasini's elder sister, Surama Biswas—Inspectress of Schools, Dacca Circle—received such a cablegram in her office located in Ramna, the 'white town' in mid-Dacca in the Bengal Presidency. It came from Macdonald Hamilton and Company, the managing agents of the Eastern and Australian Steamship Co. Ltd., London, and read as follows:[1]

---

[1] Established in 1873, the Eastern and Australian 'Mail' Steamship Company Ltd was formed under a contract between the Queensland

> Confidential. Regret advise vessel in which Miss S Biswas passenger abandoned no news yet personnel shall advise promptly any later particulars writing.

The letter that followed, confirmed the fact that the *SS Nankin* had been 'abandoned'.[2] It expressed the hope '*that those on board may have been able to leave in the lifeboats*', although no definitive information regarding the fate of the passengers was available at that time.

On 3 June 1942, another cablegram arrived, reiterating that there was '*no news yet*', merely reaffirming the earlier message of uncertainty. Confidential correspondence continued at regular intervals, attempting to provide such updates as could be obtained amid the chaos of war. Finally, on 16 December 1942, H. L. Fox of Mackinnon Mackenzie

---

Government and four British and Australian merchants to carry mail between Singapore, the Dutch East Indies, Queensland and Sydney, later extending to Hong Kong and Melbourne. After the mail contract was not renewed in 1880, the company was wound up and reconstituted as the Eastern and Australian Steamship Company Ltd. The new company focused on the Australia–Hong Kong route, later expanding services to Shanghai and Japan, carrying passengers and cargo. During the inter-war years, the company continued operating between Australia and the Far East on revised routes linking Melbourne, Sydney, Brisbane and Townsville with Rabaul, Manila, Hong Kong, Shanghai and Yokohama. By the early 1930s, the fleet had been reduced to three passenger-cargo liners—*Tanda*, *Nellore* and *Nankin*. E&A survived into the Second World War, operating between Australia and India under BI Company guidance, but suffered heavy losses: *Nankin* was captured by the Japanese in 1942, and *Nellore* and *Tanda* were lost to enemy action in 1944.

[2] When the *Nankin* was captured by the German forces, the passengers and crew were loaded on to lifeboats to board a German vessel. The captured ship instead of being 'scuttled' and destroyed had the Germans take possession of it. Being abandoned at high seas meant that *Nankin* was to henceforth fly the German flag.

Co., communicated *'information with the strictest confidence'* that *'the crew and passengers of the S.S. Nankin are safe and are prisoners of war in Japan'*.

C.T.   NO.

INDIAN POSTS AND TELEGRAPHS DEPARTMENT.

3

XF SC 79 SYDNEY 25 IRC FIL CANCEL IF DUPLICATED 31

MISS SUROMA BISWAS INSPECTRESS OF SCHOOLS DACCA

CONFINDENTIAL REGRET ADVISE VESSEL IN

WHICH MISS S BISWAS PASSENGER

ABANDONED NO NEWS YET PERSONNEL SHALL

ADVISE PROMPTLY ANY LETTER PARTICULARS WRITING

MACDONALD HAMILTON

The sequence of entries at the beginning of this telegram should be read in serial number (in the case of foreign telegrams only), office of origin, date, service instructions (if any) and number of words.

This form must accompany any enquiry respecting this telegram.

MGIPPAh.—3620—S4-9 41—16,400.

5

The cable dated 3 June 1942

From H. L. Fox
MACKINNON, MACKENZIE & CO.

TELEGRAPHIC ADDRESS :—''MACKINNONS''
TELEPHONE NO. 6100.

POST BOX NO. 163.

M. M. 335.

Calcutta, 16th December *194*2.

STRICTLY CONFIDENTIAL

Dear Miss Biswas,   Miss S. Biswas

        Further to my confidential letter of the 3rd August this year regarding your sister, Miss S. Biswas, we have received confidential information today from our Agents in Australia that they are advised that the crew and passengers of the s.s."Nankin" are safe and are prisoners of war in Japan. In passing on this information to you we have been asked by our Agents and the Naval Authorities to stress as forcefully as we can the confidential nature of this message. Will you kindly therefore treat this information with the strictest confidence.

You may advise your relations in strict confidence.

                                        Yours sincerely,

Miss S. Biswas,
    Inspectress of Schools,
        Dacca Circle,
            29 Minto Road,
                Ramna, Dacca.

The cable dated 16 December 1942

According to a pencilled diary entry by Suhasini, her homeward voyage aboard the *SS Nankin* had commenced from Sydney on 17 April 1942 at 5 p.m. (local time). The ship reached Melbourne on 20 April at 3 a.m., departing again on the evening of 24 April 1942. From there, it sailed into Fremantle on 3 May around noon, leaving port on 5 May at 7 a.m., under the command of the Master, Captain C. Stratford, with 321 people on board.

Other accounts of this passage—including the recollections of young Michael Charnaud—confirm these details, noting that among those on board were 104 passengers, including 39 women and children; 46 Lascar seamen rescued from a British tanker sunk in a bombing raid on Darwin; 26 officers (mostly Australian); and an Indian crew of 145.

The dramatic events that unfolded on the morning of Sunday, 10 May 1942, are recorded by Suhasini in terse, almost cryptic, diary notations:

> 10th unidentified plane 8AM [*sic;*] at 2.40 reappeared damaged bridge, officers' accommodation and some lifeboats. Simultaneously with air attack the ship appeared approaching over the horizon. *Nankin* altered course but enemy ship opened fire. *Nankin* guns went into action after a time we ceased fire. *Nankin* was holed low in port bow. The flag was then lowered, *Nankin* was to be scuttled after getting the passengers into the life-boats but prevented. All passengers and crew were taken aboard by the raider. A German working party boarded *Nankin*.

On 14 May, the passengers and crew captured from the *Nankin* were transferred by the Germans from the raider *Thor* to the *M.V Regensburg*. The vessel already held several prisoners from other torpedoed ships, including the British freighters *Willesden*, *Wellpark* and *Kirkpool*, as well as the Norwegian freighter *Aust*.[3]

F. W. Fox, who later documented these events, had been serving as Third Engineer on the *Kirkpool* when it was attacked and sunk north-northeast of Tristan da Cunha by the *Thor* on 10 April 1942—exactly a month before the attack on the *Nankin*. Fox had joined the *Kirkpool* on 20 January 1942, sailing from Tyneside on 31 January. Of the crew, only 30 survived and were taken aboard the *Thor*; 16 were lost. Fox and the other survivors were first transferred

---

[3] From Michael Charnaud's account, Part 4, some details of these ships are available. *Wellpark* was sunk on 30 March 1942, 1 man killed; *Willesden* was sunk 1 April 1942, with 2 men killed; *Aust* (Norwegian) sunk 3 April 1942 and *Kirkpool* sunk 10 April 1942 with the largest casualty of 16 men killed.

to the *Regensberg* in the Indian Ocean on 4 May 1942, and later, on 12 June, to the *M.V. Dresden.*

On 31 May 1942, all passengers from the *Nankin*, along with some additional prisoners, had already been transshipped to the *Dresden*. The Second World War papers of Fox[4] corroborate the entries recorded by Suhasini in her exercise book. Throughout much of June, the *Dresden* steamed towards Japan, travelling via the Sunda Strait,[5] the Java Sea and perhaps west of the Philippines. The destination, kept secret by the Germans until the last moment, was revealed only when the ship anchored in Tokyo Bay on 23 June 1942, entering Yokohama harbour the following day.

On 3 July 1942, the prisoners were transferred to the *Rameses*, along with prisoners from the *Pagiatellos*, and on 10 July 1942 they were 'officially' handed over by the Germans and placed under Japanese custody. This voyage to Japan as prisoners of war has been documented by several first-person accounts, which together enable a reconstruction of the sequence of events.

These civilians, including Suhasini, could have had no idea of what was happening to them or where they were headed as they voyaged on the rough seas. Suhasini was thankful, like the others, for being alive and trusted the Lord with her destiny. She was grateful for three things: that they were allowed to retrieve their personal belongings from the *Nankin*; that the Germans treated them humanely; and that they were given adequate food.

------

[4] The Second World War papers of F. W. Fox of Gateshead-on-Tyne, County Durham, England (P463) held in the Imperial War Museum, London.

[5] The Sunda Strait was notorious around March 1942 for the battle that sunk two Allied cruisers when these encountered a Japanese naval attack. The route chosen as a passage from the Indian Ocean through the Java Sea into the Pacific was under Axis control.

Robert Murphy, in his dissertation[6] on the internment camps asks several pertinent questions about what the trade-offs might have been concerning civilians captured by German raider ships—even in previous months and far away from Japan. What were the terms of the German–Japanese agreement concerning these civilians, if any? Why did the German officials, during the handing over, promise to keep in touch with the prisoners? Under what circumstances did they acquire the valuables and currency that the captives carried, and take these into their safe custody? For instance, Madeline Charnaud handed over a sealed packet of jewellery to a German officer.

However, this ambivalent status would not have been apparent to the internees at that point, as they were overwhelmed and confused by events over which they had no control whatsoever. As far as the prisoners were concerned, they were in Japan, surrounded by Japanese commandants and personnel, and therefore visibly under Japanese surveillance. Whether they were legally German POWs being detained in Japan, or Japanese POWs, remained an unanswered question—one that had serious consequences, for the outside world was unaware of the existence of this particular camp for almost three years.

Oblivious to their ambiguous status amid the larger geopolitical maelstrom, the survivors, handed over to the Japanese by 7 p.m. on 10 July 1942, were herded on to a motor bus to the railway station and then put on a train to Fukushima the same day. Boarding a 'prisoner train' with no idea of what awaited them at the end of the journey was nerve-wracking. The wait in the train till 9.45 p.m. was as

---

[6] R.G. Murphy's dissertation titled 'The Fukushima Civil Internment Camp, 1942–1945', was submitted to the School of East Asian Studies, Faculty of Social Sciences, University of Sheffield in 2006. This was a requirement for the MA in Japanese Language & Society (by Distance Learning) offered by the university.

frightening as having to vacate the electric train at Ueno and shift to a steam train well past 11 p.m. Following a sparse meal at 3.30 a.m., they reached Fukushima station at 7.40 the next morning. After a sleepless night, tired and exhausted, the prisoners finally arrived at their destination—a prison camp—at about 9.00 a.m. the next day (11 July 1942). It was a hot, sultry day during one of the hottest summers recorded in Japan. From the railway station, the women and children were put on a bus, while the men walked across the small town into the countryside to reach the camp, set up in a commandeered convent. They were informed by a Japanese official that they would henceforth be under the authority of a Special Branch of the Police of the Fukushima Prefecture.

The account of a fellow internee, A. C. Round,[7] and the diary of F. W. Fox flesh out Suhasini's spare jottings, noting the sequence of harrowing transfers even after the prisoners disembarked from the *Rameses*.

Fukushima Prefecture, located on Japan's eastern Pacific coast at the southernmost part of the Tōhoku region, was a mountainous region with lakes and paddy fields. The convent—with a spire and cross atop the building—where the prisoners were taken, was a fairly new construction at the time, a modern Gothic-style building set within

----

[7] A.C. Round was on the freighter *Kirkpool* when it was sunk. His diary maintained at the Fukushima camp was a closely-written account in what was essentially a small pad made out of slivers of paper and cardboard from boxes presumably distributed through the International Red Cross. The pad was roughly stitched together at the top and is part of the Imperial War Museum (91/31/1). In the foreword, Round writes, '*At the time of writing, I find myself enduring a long imprisonment in an enemy country, and having much time on my hands I desire to take the opportunity of describing the experience which resulted in my being here. What I shall write will resolve itself into an eye-witness account...*' (21 March 1945)

grounds of about three acres and surrounded by a six-foot solid brick-and-mortar wall. There were secure wrought-iron gates with sentry boxes. A French-Canadian order of nuns, the Sisters of Notre Dame de Protection, had lived there before the place was taken over by the Japanese government after December 1941, when Japan came into conflict with the Western Allies, forcing the nuns to hastily vacate.

The March 2011 undersea earthquake off the Pacific coast of Tōhoku, measuring 9.0 on the Richter scale, and the powerful tsunami that followed, devastated large parts of Fukushima. The then Japanese Prime Minister Naoto Kan described it as 'the toughest and the most difficult crisis for Japan' since the Second World War. Fukushima was once again in the news with extensive damage to its nuclear power plants and mass evacuation amid fears of radioactive exposure. The earthquake caused irreparable damage to the convent, to which the Sisters of Notre Dame de Protection had returned soon after the prisoners left in mid-September 1945. The destroyed convent had to be demolished, thereby erasing the physical trace of the Second World War POW camp.

Hungry and parched after the long and anxious journey, the internees were told to gather in the convent's assembly hall to be addressed by the Camp Commandant. The resident Commandant at the camp was apparently a lower-ranking police officer in charge of the guards. He may have been implementing orders from a senior officer at the Prefecture who rarely set foot in the camp to inspect conditions. The message conveyed that afternoon by the Commandant was interpreted by a man who would later prove to be manipulative. The ambiguity surrounding the legal status of the prisoners—as internees held either under German or Japanese authority—proved instrumental in the camp being declared a 'Secret Establishment'. It soon became apparent that neither the Red Cross nor the Neutral Powers were informed of the camp's existence for several months. For the prisoners, this meant no access to basic comforts and no communication with the outside world. They were entirely at the mercy of petty Japanese guards who exercised authoritarian control and were inordinately cruel.

The ordeal on the high seas had thus ended only to give way to another, and the future seemed deeply uncertain. The prisoners had only hope to cling on as they endured and survived each day as it unfolded.

3

Destination Fukushima

Suhasini had embarked on the *Nankin* from Sydney on 17 April 1942, excited about her homeward voyage to India. Little had she anticipated the dramatic events on the high seas that would keep her away from home not just for months but for years. The nightmarish experiences en route testify to how the lives of ordinary men and women were directly affected by the global conflict. Here were Suhasini and her shipmates—men, women and children—who had sailed across continents, being shifted from one marine vessel to another before finally reaching Yokohama harbour, a distance of more than 9,370 km (5,822 miles). Just a week short of three months later, the shipload of captives was back on terra firma. The relief was palpable, though they were entirely unsure of what to expect in this new phase.

After their arrival at the convent, it became clear that for the several months until the war ended, they would be held in this remote corner of Japan as civilian prisoners of war, hidden from the world and agencies like the International Red Cross. The choice of location for the prison camp was apparently well considered—the virtually unknown region had once been called Michi-no-ku, meaning 'a land far removed from the road', and had not come under the Japanese Yamato Court, which wielded imperial power around the fourth century. Given the journey they had made and the destination they had reached, there must have been a complex mix of primarily negative feelings—anguish, fear and insecurity—amongst the prisoners.

The Fukushima Committee Report, submitted by a group of internees to the International Red Cross after the war, describes the convent building thus:

> The building was excellent, a two-storied ferro-concrete structure with an attic above the upper storey and a small basement. It was divided into two sections, one accommodating the men internees and the other the women and children internees, which were separated by fireproof steel doors. The administrative offices, the two mess rooms for internees, a large hall, the kitchen, a laundry room, the guards' mess room and some of the women internees' quarters occupied the ground floor; the internee' quarters and a chapel occupied the upper storey; the attic was used as a lumber room and was never opened for use by internees; the furnaces and boilers of an efficient central heating installation and a small storeroom occupied the basement...[1]

Ironically, the POW camp was located in the Convent building, where the Japanese commandants had demarcated shared spaces that allowed no sense of privacy or belonging, adding to an already unsettling frame of mind. The attic, the basement, the administrative office rooms, and the waiting room comprised 'no-entry' zones for the internees, intimidating and frightening in an unfamiliar and alien environment. These would become sites of punishment and abuse in the months to follow.

What it was to be a prisoner of war could only have become apparent to the internees as they started settling down in the camp, initially yielding to moments of uneasy relief that their days on the threatening high seas—packed

---

[1] http://www.mansell.com/pow_resources/camplists/sendai/fukushima/report_1.html, accessed on 22 March 2025.

into claustrophobic ship cabins—had been replaced by what seemed, at first, to be more spacious confinement in a Convent building with its own grounds and garden. Radio officer Malcolm Engreby Scott, a British national and a fellow internee at Fukushima, reported that the building they were housed in stood 'in grounds of approximately three acres, most of which is vegetable garden with the exception of a concrete exercise ground of about 40 x 15 yards'.[2]

However, there were numerous restrictions even on catching a breath of fresh air in the garden, walking down the compound paths, or looking over the wall to glimpse the outside world and the villagers passing by. Suhasini notes in her exercise book: *'Our activities are so limited that life is sure to be monotonous. The space to move about out of doors is restricted just to a few square yards for fixed times in the day and that too not even everyday so that one does not wonder at the rheumatic pains we suffer from.'*

Camp records indicate that the rooms were somewhat cramped, with at least three internees assigned to living quarters measuring only eight by twelve feet. The six larger rooms accommodated up to twenty persons. Once the *tatami* or rice-straw sleeping mats measuring six feet by three feet, were spread out on the floor, there was hardly any space to move around. The bedding allotted to each internee consisted of a two-inch-thick *tatami*, a thin mattress, a cotton quilt, a sheet, and—eventually—pillows in place of the packed-straw headrest.

Sanitary arrangements were fairly adequate during the first part of the stay, but over time, as the camp authorities failed to carry out even minor repairs, several taps, sinks, baths, and lavatories became unusable. Although the

____

[2] https://www.cofepow.org.uk/armed-forces-stories-list/fukushima-civilian-internment-camp-japan-june-1945. Accessed on 8 October 2025.

convent had an efficient heating system, the internees still faced bitter cold as coal supplies dwindled; hot water was provided only once a week. There was also the persistent problem of limited access to soap and the difficulty of washing clothes, both of which made daily life quite miserable for the inmates.

In his entries of 11 and 13 July 1942, Round summarised the camp environment: *'Comfortable quarters, small and very poor meals. Guards officious and cantankerous... Rooms and beds very comfortable. Nice building, food terrible.'*

Suhasini, meanwhile, had scribbled in her notebook stoic thoughts and idealistic expectations that several of the internees shared during the early days of their confinement:

> An internee has to be in confinement in the country of an enemy for political, precautional reasons and for no wrong committed by the individual. It is a mere accident that our life had to be passed as an internee in Fukushima Japan [as internees]. Consequently we came with the impression that not hindering the discipline of the camp would make for the country's interest and pleasure and privileges not be denied to us and we would strive our level best to help in the efficient administration by our good conduct, since we cherish no personal grudge against any under whose charge we were placed.

The early expectations of the internees and the promises held out to them initially created an enabling and positive psychological environment. The experience of being a 'prisoner' was new for all, and each one felt a sense of community and togetherness that arose from essentially collective suffering. Although the one hundred and forty internees were a heterogeneous group of transnational citizens—different in race, culture, religion, and nationality, with inevitable differences in personality—they bonded over their common fate. Every individual was coping with emerging conditions that required daily adjustments to the physical environment, an acute reliance on mental stamina, and the overall courage to endure.

From the very beginning, a sense of lack haunted the prisoners—a lack of hygiene, sustainable food, basic comforts, engaging pastimes or conversations, and most importantly, any personal freedom. Inadequate and unpalatable food remained a major hardship for the internees throughout their stay, and each of them suffered severely. Suhasini, in her marginalia, prays for the strength to cope with the pangs of hunger that physically undermined their attempts to maintain an unflagging morale, which was itself a survival tactic. She lived through the physical discomfort and mental trauma by immersing herself in her deep faith in God, by interacting with the other internees, and by helping them manage the trying conditions.

In the initial days of their internment, all personal possessions were confiscated. Suhasini's prized possession and spiritual companion—a Bengali copy of Rabindranath Tagore's *Gitanjali*[3]—had been smuggled into the camp. The Japanese guards were told that it was a Bible, and while permission to keep it was likely to have been granted reluctantly, Suhasini made the book her source of solace and sustenance throughout her years as a prisoner. She used the *Gitanjali* as a personal diary, scribbling observations, confessions and insights with the stub of a pencil that she had picked up—luckily unseen by any of the guards— during the mandatory morning drill for all prisoners.

Each day at dawn, the Convent bell in the main hallway was rung, calling prisoners to put away their bedding, change out of night clothes, dress, and line up along the corridor for roll call. Japanese guards would bark out the

---

[3] Rabindranath Tagore was the first Asian to have been awarded the Nobel Prize for literature in 1913 for his book of poems *Gitanjali: Song Offerings,* an English translation of 103 songs from the original Bengali version.

identification numbers printed on small wooden pieces that each internee had to wear around the neck. A similar roll call took place at the end of each day.

By now, it is clear that settling down in the camp was far from easy. The internees' emotional trauma intensified when the Chief of Fukushima's Special Police visited the camp on 1 August 1942 and announced that they would have to sign a paper, on oath to God, affirming that they would obey all camp rules. A cyclostyled copy of these rules was found among Suhasini's papers, and new rules continued to be added at the whim of the guards, with the prohibitions eventually reaching 173. Internees were also 'politely informed to wait their pleasure for anything required and not try to demand things', a statement that clearly set the tone for how camp discipline would be maintained.

While these already traumatised internees were trying to come to terms with the atmosphere of pettiness and control that the camp rules sought to enforce, the deaths that occured in the following months cast a deep pall of gloom over them. The emotional impact was intensely depressing for all, especially the children. The grief of losing campmates so soon after internment made the men and women helplessly angry at the total absence of compassion shown by the guards and authorities.

Due to the absence of any medical assistance, the camp witnessed two deaths in the early days. V. W. Hemy died at 9.25 p.m. on 15 August 1942 from stomach ulcers that could easily have been treated. The funeral service and burial took place on 17 August on a hill a short distance from the camp. About a month later, Nicol MacIntyre, a 64-year-old merchant seaman, suffered a stroke and, according to camp records, was forced to work in the hot sun for the next two days before he died at four minutes past midnight on 13 September. He was cremated on 15 September 1942. Medical aid was never arranged, and the entire episode was handled casually and callously by the authorities.

THE RULES OF THE FUKUSHIMA INTERNMENT CAMP

ROLL CALL.

1. Must not get up before first bell.
2. Must be fully dressed for roll call.
3. Must not wear dressing gown to roll call.
4. Beds must be folded before roll call.
5. Must not smile at roll call.
6. Must remember off in Nipponese.

WASHING AND BATHING.

7. Must only wash face, feet and hands daily.
8. Must use wooden shoes in lavatories.
9. No clothes must be washed on Sundays.
10. Must not use hot water for washing clothes.
11. Must not wash after roll call at night.
12. Must not waste water.
13. Must not pour water over ourselves.
14. A number must get into the same tub of water on bath days an[d] [must]
    not pour water over ourselves.
15. Must not go out to clothes line except at stated times.
16. Must not hang clothes in bathroom.
17. Children must be bathed in mothers bath time.

MEALS.

18. Must not exceed 15 minutes for each meal.
19. Must not take bread to our rooms.
20. Must not keep cutlery or crockery in rooms.
21. Must not look sliding windows of dining rooms.
22. Must not close dining room windows when the guard has opened [them].
23. Must not enter kitchen.
24. Must not wear head covering during meals.
25. Must not talk to kitchen staff on duty.
26. Anyone breaking crockery loses a days meals.
27. Must not have cutlery washed by kitchen staff.
28. Must all be waiting downstairs behind iron door for [meal bell to r...]

SMOKING.

29. Must not smoke before roll call in the evening and a[fter ro]l[l call]
    at night.
30. Must not smoke in corridors.
31. Must not put ashtrays on sleeping mats.
32. Must not claim cigarette ration if a non-smoker.

MEN INTERNEES.

33. Must not wave or smile at the men.
34. Must not communicate in anyway except throught the [off]ice.

OFFICIAL.

35. Must not try to be friendly with guards.
36. Must always do anything any guard orders at any time.
37. Must bow to every guard on meeting.
38. Must not bow with hands in pockets.
39. Must remove head covering when bowing.
40. Must bow when entering or leaving office.
41. Must not wear head covering into office.
42. Must not wear coats into office.
43. Must refer to a guard as "Tai-jiu", sergeant as "Bu[ ]o[ ]" [and]
    the Japanese people as "Nippon - Jiu".

GARDEN, [next ...]

The first page of the camp rules

Though death is a natural part of life, in these circumstances the two fatalities were ominous signs of a bleak future— one marked by severe physical endurance, psychological scars and emotional distress for those who had witnessed the events. The physical and emotional conditions in the camp became increasingly stressful, heightened by the constant fear of corporal punishment and a pervasive sense of utter abjection. None of the usual clinical parameters of psychological care—such as understanding, kindness, adequate meals, or any form of de-stressing the environment—were available to the internees. Each person was left to his or her own strategies to cope with the situation during these early months of captivity.

4

A 'Taste' of Camp Life

Camp life at Fukushima unfolded under the harsh enforcement of the invidious 'Rules of the Fukushima Internment Camp' by cantankerous guards. The first set of 133 rules were listed under various categories, each defining a particular form of control[1] designed to stifle all forms of personal freedom and independence. In many ways, these rules reflected the fear and anxiety of those who wielded the power to hold civilians as prisoners. The guards were frequently abusive and often resorted to physical violence as a way of asserting their authority. One of the most common punishments was face-slapping, which could escalate into hurtful punching, even involving

---

[1] Foucault argues in *Discipline and Punish: The Birth of the Prison* (1975) that Western penal systems shifted from public spectacles of punishment and torture to more hidden forms of surveillance and control. He shows how social structures shape the ways in which power is exercised and maintained. In the case of the Fukushima civilian camp, the Japanese guards and commandants relied on systematic physical force to assert their authority. At times, notions of civility and justice as understood in the Western world, were unfamiliar in a context where the Emperor's authority remained unquestioned. Alongside physical violence, other methods of punishment, including deprivation and mental torture, were also widespread in the camp.

women prisoners. Kneeling for hours on the hard wooden floor—sometimes for most of the day—was another frequently inflicted torture. Standing outside in the heat or cold with a bucket of water that could not be put down was a punishment often used for men the guards perceived as 'recalcitrant'. In this new moral and political environment, the rules did not just uphold justice but instead reiterated the right to punish. Control and regulation were central, and those in power maintained their authority through force, fear, and repeated corporal punishment.

As seen in the image shared in the previous chapter, almost every rule on the sheet began with a 'Must not...', reflecting the authoritarian control imposed on prisoners, who were not criminals but ordinary civilians caught in the turmoil of war. The ordeal began with the very first waking moment—Rule Number 1 reads, 'Must not wake up before first bell', followed by five rules about getting fully dressed and folding the beds before the daily morning roll call. This was followed by periodic checks and a final lining up before going to bed, all part of a system aimed at enforcing discipline in a potentially restive population.

According to the internees, there was a perceptible decline in their status and treatment once the Germans handed them over to the Japanese, who then became their custodians. Robert Murphy in his dissertation (2006, 15–16) writes:

> The sense of betrayal, a kind of racially-tinged sense that one 'civilised' white race was abandoning helpless and injured civilians to the barbaric Japanese, was strong when the prisoners were handed over in Yokohama on 10th July 1942. Internees noted that even the German crews were uncomfortable. Some felt that the arrangement would be temporary, and that the Germans would ensure better treatment for their captives than was commonly believed normal from the Japanese, until exchange arrangements with the Allies could be concluded.

The tactics applied by the Japanese may be described as an 'economy of suspended rights', in which '[T]he body according to this penalty is caught up in a system of constraints and privations, obligations and prohibitions' (Foucault 1975, 11). In the camp, loss of liberty was inextricably linked to bodily deprivations—rationed food, withdrawal of food as punishment, sexual constraints, surveillance over personal hygiene, and corporal punishment, even for children.

Daily routines became inordinately difficult. Under the sub-heading 'Washing and Bathing' in the list of rules, inmates faced strict restrictions on usage of water and were required to follow the Japanese practice of communal bathing, where several people used the same bathtub. Maintaining personal hygiene was extremely challenging, as bathing, washing, and laundering were heavily controlled. Fox noted in his diary entry of 31 January 1943 that the inmates were *given soap—1 piece 2 3/8" × 1 3/16" × ½" to be divided between 3 men for washing clothes and bathing. This works out at 1/3rd per man.* On 4 December 1942, Round recorded: *'One dessert spoon of soap issued to each prisoner. Insufficient.'* Two days later, on 6 December 1942, he added, *'One cake of soap given for 95 men to bathe with. Only done 30 men.'*

It is clear that the shortage of soap and basic supplies was unlikely to improve until the existence of the camp became known outside, two years after its secret establishment, allowing the International Red Cross to intervene with assistance. Suhasini's notebooks often include inventory-like lists of essential items, possibly kept in collective custody. Some of these charts also contain the names of internees alongside columns noting the food or toiletry items being stored by fellow prisoners.

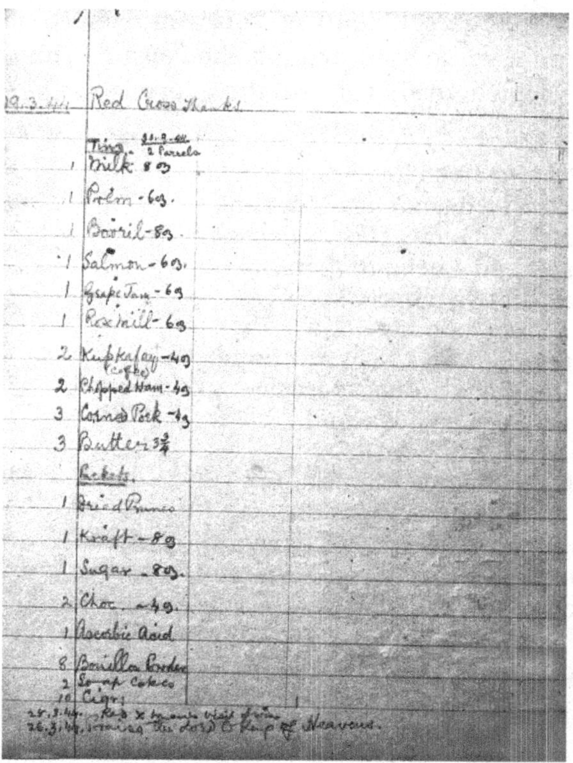

*Pages from Suhasini's notebook containing inventory-like
lists of essentials*

A spirit of sharing and mutual trust became essential for
survival in an unfamiliar and often hostile environment.
Miss S. Curtis[2] (likely a pseudonym adopted by one of the

---

[2] The seven-page manuscript appears to be a set of transcriptions
made, most probably in 1945, by the matron of a military hospital
in Ceylon. It includes four poems written by unidentified civilian
internees from the Fukushima camp in Japan, reflecting on their
lives in captivity and on their eventual liberation. It also contains
a two-page report dated December 1942, written by three female
internees, describing an incident in which Japanese authorities
attempted to force them to brand their children as punishment for
a minor offence. These documents were presumably shown to Miss

internees for safety) captured this atmosphere with sharp humour in a verse built around the refrain 'The things we learned', which wryly reflects the everyday experiences of life in the camp. 'She' writes:

> Well we've been 3 years in prison
> Gosh we've been 3 years in clink
> Haven't had a meal that's decent
> Haven't had a drop to drink.
> Haven't had a whisky soda,
> Just a smell of body odour
> But we've always kept one hope.
> In a life that's minus soap,
> The things we've learned.
>
> We've had chilblain initiation
> And constant constipation
> Sometimes earthquakes gave us jitters
> Sometimes pumpkins gave us squitters
> We can do 'kioski' fine (stand to attention)
> And 'Meni neu' into line (hands on hips)
> We can 'bang' now quite snappy (roll call)
> And 'kaeri' to make them happy (bow)
> The things we've learned.
>
> We can pinch and we can steal,
> And no turn of conscience feel,
> We can smile a friendly grin,
> With a heart as black as sin,
> We can eat the leek that stinks
> And take dishwater for our drinks,
> And we think it only just,
> If we receive a daily crust.
> The things we've learned.
>
> At dominoes we do excel,
> And at chess we are quite swell,

Curtis by a former internee who was receiving medical treatment in Ceylon after liberation.

At judo we are really class,
And we go right thro' the 'class'
We know Spanish, shorthand, Greek,
We have lessons every week,
Chinese, German and Malay
All helpless the dreary day,
The things we've learned.

We can read each sign and token,
And find each fine promise broken,
We can stand the lack of Fags,
And bellies like empty bags,
We can do so many things
This life out each talent brings,
But we do not need our knolls,
To tell us they're simply —
Gosh! The things we've learned.

Mealtimes were carefully monitored by the guards, and the inadequate, substandard food remained a legitimate and persistent grievance. Most internees barely survived on the meagre rations, and by the end of the ordeal, many were skeletal, frail, and severely emaciated. Camp records note that Suhasini had lost 25 pounds (around 12 kilograms) between July 1942 and her release in August/September 1945.

The strict and overbearing 'Mealtime Rules and Regulations' appeared absurd when set against the reality of the rations—food that was barely sufficient to sustain life. The rules read:

MEALS

18. Must not exceed 15 minutes for each meal.
19. Must not take bread to our rooms.
20. Must not keep cutlery or crockery in rooms.
21. Must not look [out of] sliding windows of dining rooms.

22. Must not close dining room windows when the guard has opened them.
23. Must not enter kitchen.
24. Must not wear head covering during meals.
25. Must not talk to kitchen staff on duty.
26. Anyone breaking crockery loses a day's meals.
27. Must not have cutlery washed by kitchen staff.
28. Must all be waiting downstairs behind iron door for meal bell to ring.

The meagre and often spoiled food frequently resulted in illness. On 21 August 1942, Round recorded in his diary: '*Ten men down with bad stomachs. Due to bad meat served to us. Women also sick.*' The basic daily food rations consisted of a small portion of bread and watered-down tea without milk or sugar. Both Round and Fox marked 29 October 1942 as a '*Big day*', noting with surprise and relief that the prisoners were given three slices of bread for their meal—'*a big stride in the food question*', as Fox put it.

For prisoners deprived of even a single decent meal, small variations in the diet became noteworthy events. Receiving liver paté instead of jam for breakfast, a little butter for breakfast, or having a fruit for dinner on 8 November 1942—something they had not seen since their confinement—were significant enough to be carefully recorded in diaries and journals. Sometimes a change in the Camp Captain or Commandant could be detected through slight improvements in the food. On 29 July 1943, after such a change of guard, each man received four boiled sweets, and by August there was a modest increase in fruit and food in the daily rations.

A moment of genuine rejoicing came on 15 March 1944. '*Big day. Camp gone wild. At last the Red Cross have found us out. 35 food parcels from American Red Cross arrived*', Round wrote. After nearly twenty months, the International Red Cross had finally discovered the camp's secret location. Just a few days later, on 19 March 1944, each internee received a parcel—*'what a feed!'*, Fox exclaimed. The arrival of this first trace of international aid brought a ray of hope, signalling the possibility of communication with the world beyond the camp's boundaries.

Fox, like Suhasini, noted the contents of the first Red Cross parcel that generated such rejoicing:

> 1lb tin of klim (powdered milk)
> 3 ¾ tin of butter
> Tin of jam
> Tin of salmon
> Meat patte
> Pkt coffee
> Pkt soap
> Chocolate
> Tins spam, prunes, cheese
> Sugar
> Tablet corned beef
> 30 packets cigarettes

The women internees at Fukushima had, in March 1944, drafted and submitted a letter to the International Red Cross describing the day-to-day conditions at the camp. Under the heading 'Food', the letter reported the following:

> Food: day's diet, inadequate, unvaried. Breakfast 1 bun (6 ozs), 1 cup weak tea (no milk or sugar). Lunch 1 bun, 1 cup weak tea. Supper 1bun, 1 cup weak tea, 1 small plate of stew consisting of a little meat, rice and barley or vegetables, the total weighing 3 or 3 ½ ozs. Days of visiting officials two meals—larger than ordinary meals. Occasionally small tangerine or fruit in season—no fat, no oil, no calcium or vitamins.

Among the several forms of deprivation that were routine in the camp, the lack of food was perhaps the most mentally and physically debilitating. Healthy and nutritious meals remained a distant dream; there were even days when the internees received no bread for lunch and supper because nearly 500 buns had gone sour and were returned to the bakery. The arrival of the Red Cross parcels after March 1944 generated widespread excitement, yet by September a growing concern spread through the camp as food shortages across Japan threatened to further reduce their already meagre supplies. In such bleak conditions, the distribution of Red Cross parcels became the internees' sole source of hope.

Given the general scarcity of food, one common form of punishment for transgressing any of the 133 camp rules was the withdrawal of a meal. Those addicted to cigarettes often bartered their food meal for cigarettes, and Round, in a diary entry for 25 July 1945, writes in utter anguish:

> Oh to see the war end. I haven't had a bit of stew for quite a time. Still receiving 3 ½ small buns and hot water for breakfast, lunch, tea. The bread is very dirty, tasteless and insufficient. Even so I am thankful for it as it is our only diet. Stop our bread and our weary hearts stop. Oh! Yankees come! Come! Come! There are so many gruesome sights in the camp. Walking skeletons.

A statistical synopsis of the unvarying and far-from-nourishing meal rations appears as a refrain after almost every date-wise diary entry in Round's diary. In contrast, Suhasini's observations were more reticent. Although she did not fail to note the *'the insufficient food both in quality and quantity'*, her notebook reveals a different emphasis: she seems to have assumed the role of a careful custodian, meticulously setting aside food and other small supplies to be shared on special occasions such as birthdays and anniversaries.

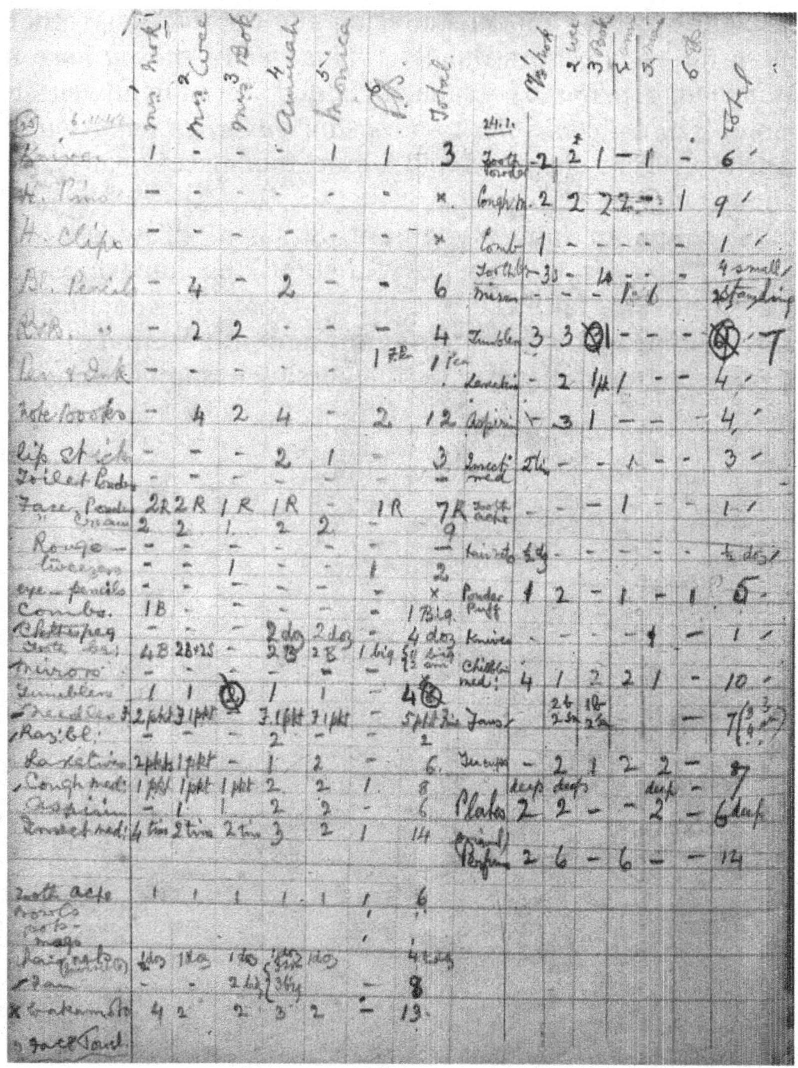

Suhasini's diary entry meticulously recording supplies set aside for special occasions

Alongside a Bengali song (no. 5) in the *Gitanjali*—a verse that takes the form of an intimate prayer for mental strength and the spirit to endure suffering and deprivation, rather than for rescue from danger (*bipade more raksha koro e nohe mor prarthana*)—Suhasini added a brief handwritten note: '*Truly, I can claim to have said this when hungry and parched...*' The entry is dated 5 June, though the year is not indicated.

Throughout her internment, Suhasini drew on her inner reserves of faith to withstand the hardships of camp life. This faith was not directed toward a specifically Christian God, but towards a non-denominational divine presence that, for her, quietly oversaw human destiny.

5

Of Control and Punishment

It was the German naval forces that had initially captured this socially and racially diverse group of civilians and ship crew in the South Atlantic and Indian Ocean region. Under the Geneva Convention of 1929, Germany should have remained responsible for those taken into custody. However, through a peculiar chain of events, they ultimately ended up as prisoners in a Japanese internment camp in Fukushima. Researchers have found no official documents in German or Japanese archives that clarify the reasons for this unusual and highly ambiguous arrangement in which the internees eventually found themselves.

Across Japan—in Tokyo, Osaka, Nagasaki and Fukuoka—there were other camps and sub-camps holding Allied prisoners. Conditions in these camps were, by most accounts, comparable in their brutality and the harsh treatment routinely inflicted on inmates.

The bitter irony of the Fukushima incarceration lay in the fact that these internees were not criminals, murderers, or thieves. They were law-abiding civilians of their respective countries, classified as enemies by the Germans and Japanese simply because they belonged to Allied nations at war with the Axis powers.

Summarising and logically deciphering the internee experience in Fukushima, Suhasini in her characteristically understated idiom wrote in her notebook:

An internee has to be in confinement in the country of the enemy for political, precautional reasons and for no wrong committed by the individual. It is a mere accident that our life has to be passed as an internee in Fukushima Japan. Consequently we came with the impression that pleasures and privileges safe for the country's interest and not hindering the discipline of the camp would not be denied to us and we would strive our level best to help in the efficient administration by our good conduct, since we cherish no personal grudge against any under whose charge we were placed. With regret I say, we have felt we are prisoners in a prison within a prison. Life has been very difficult and trying.

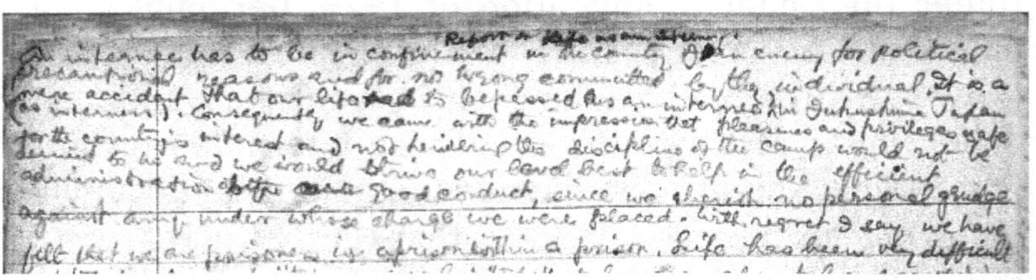

The page from Suhasini's notebook with the above quote

Had freedom been permitted within the confines of the camp, the circumstances might have unfolded differently. The living accommodation was cramped and lacked privacy, with three internees assigned to each small room, with not an inch to spare once the sleeping mats, or *tatamis*, were rolled out on the floor. Rooms a little larger in size were furnished with a table, a chair and built-in wardrobes. However, the rules dictated that during the day *'Beds must be kept folded, piled in one corner and covered with blanket... Must not put up mosquito nets or make beds before night roll call'*.

It is quite evident that the imprisonment Suhasini describes was marked by severe physical confinement, restricted access to even the limited space available. However, this spatial restriction differed from that of an actual prison, as the internees were not locked in individual cells. Instead, a subtle form of segmentation operated within the living quarters—a freezing and disciplining of internal space—with a clear demarcation between the rooms and the outer garden. The camp's rules, or disciplinary regime, enforced a pervasive system of surveillance under which each individual lost the liberty of movement, rest, and basic bodily autonomy. The constraints on the internees including the following:

44. Must go out when ordered (unless sick).
45. Must not come in without permission of guard.
46. Must not lie and sleep out of doors.
47. Must not look over the wall.
48. Must not walk beyond limits stated [by] guard on duty.
49. Must not pick flowers, fruits or vegetables.
50. Must not take blankets out of doors.
51. Must not take chairs into the garden.
52. Must not sit or stand on grass.
53. Must sit on paths.
54. Children must not urinate in garden.
55. May not go inside to the lavatory without permission of the guards.
56. Children must wash feet outside before entering if not wearing shoes.
57. No bread must be eaten in the garden.

The regulatory function of these rules was to control even the most trivial details of daily life and movement, to locate each individual, fix them in a specific place, and thereby exercise power over their interactions with others.

The 142 internees in the camp comprised a cosmopolitan mix—British civilians and seamen, Chinese, Australian, South and West Africans, Spaniards, Greek seamen, British Arabs, an Armenian and a British Indian (Suhasini). This diverse range of customs, cultures, languages, and sensibilities could easily have turned the camp into a proverbial Tower of Babel. Yet the extremity of their circumstances demanded cohesion—a merging of individual identities into a unified community capable of cohabiting.

The Japanese authorities, on the other hand, sought to intercept all forms of exchange and dismantle any sense of communal solidarity through multiple surveillance techniques designed to isolate individuals. Suhasini continues her summary of life in Fukushima thus:

> In addition to these trying circumstances the hard times that we have had to go through during the first half of this period has to be mentioned for an adequate idea of our internment life. The harsh and brutal treatment from the officers had a deplorable effect on our nerves. We were treated and punished like criminals several times. For want of proper, sensible and fixed routine for our movements, we were never at ease and that has told greatly on our health.

The constraints were nerve-wracking, the camp rules unrelenting, and the *'want of proper, sensible fixed routine'* left the internees with a gnawing sense of unease that steadily eroded both mental and physical health. The authority wielded by the camp guards and the Commandant manifested in the forceful enforcement of rules, the deliberate suspension of all rights to privacy, disciplinary actions for even perceived misdemeanours, and routine displays of physical intimidation intended to infuse a sense of fear. To undermine any semblance of camp solidarity, the guards frequently singled out individuals for exemplary punishment, thereby ensuring prompt obedience in the future.

For instance, on 2 October 1944, Cyril Hugh Walker (a 31-year-old British electrical engineer) was slapped and punished for blowing kisses to his girlfriend, one of the women internees—likely 26-year-old Clara Lavender Yates, whose parents were also detained as British civilian internees in Fukushima. On 23 October 1944, all the men were made to stand at attention outdoors from 2–5 p.m. for refusing to run during that afternoon's drill. On 3 March 1945, inmates Kie and Boboy were taken downstairs and slapped for smoking in the corridor. On 14 April 1945, Cecil Saunders (46-year-old Briton and General Manager of Anglo-Iranian Oil) had a bucket of water tied to his wrists and was forced to stand under the bell as punishment.

Round's diary captures these daily indignities vividly. In an entry dated 19 July 1945, he wrote, *'Slit-eyes the guard took the little wooden rifle I made for young Howard and broke it in pieces. Oh how long will it be before the Japs treat us properly? Finished making a card for Howard. His birthday tomorrow.'*[1]

Again, on 29 July, Round witnessed the same guard Slit Eyes[2] bullying ten-year-old Howard, pressing the child

---

[1] Howard Gunstone was under seven years old when he was taken prisoner along with his mother Helen Guy. One of the early incidents (December 1942) in which Howard threw a ball which unfortunately broke a glass pane in the front door invited brutal disciplinary action by the camp authorities that haunted him and his friends Graham Sparkes (aged ten) and Michael Charnaud (aged eleven) for a long time to come. In this instance, Howard was perhaps just turning a year older.

[2] The internees had their own private nicknames for the camp commandant or guards. Just a year into their internment, a new Commandant, Captain Mitsuhashi Yosio arrived. He was assigned the nickname 'Pumpkin Controller' as he was obsessed with the pumpkins grown in the garden adjoining the camp. Then there was Fishface, Lanky and Slit Eyes.

slowly to the floor while explaining something in Japanese. When Round confronted him, the guard released Howard and instead approached him aggressively. Reflecting on these atrocities, and attempting to console himself, Round wrote in his diary the next day, 30 July:

> It is difficult to lead a Christian life in the position and conditions in which we live. All around us lie snares and pitfalls. It is only by the Grace of our Heavenly Father who sees all things that we are able to stand and go on despite the very bitter disappointments which glare at us almost continually. Myself, I have the weakness of taking things casually and free and easy and taking no thought of anything and go on recklessly taking no thought of what I should do. Just like yesterday when I had the nerve to go and stop the guard who was bullying little Howard. It is this free and easy style which leads one to great trouble and difficulties and is apt to interfere with God's plans for my life.

One brutal incident that deeply shocked the entire camp in the early days was the assault on 41-year-old Florence Pat Thoms—a British housewife and the women's representative—on 2 July 1943, a day Round described as a *'really black day'*. One of the Japanese guards punched her, threw her onto the tiled porch, and kicked her repeatedly in the body and face. Suhasini also makes a passing reference to this event in her copy of *Gitanjali*. On page 16, amid a series of cryptic entries about camp happenings, she mentions the 'arrogant' camp commander and his treatment of Annie Law, an elderly missionary, and others; it is here that she adds the remark *'the night incident of the ill-fated Mrs. Thoms'*.

The internees were united in their shock and horror at the attack. Fox notes in his diary that *'tonight was the nearest we were to rioting'*. The following day, the Camp Commandant was informed about the assault and appeared shocked, *'feigning great sympathy'*. Sensing the mood in the camp, the guard who had attacked Mrs. Thoms was suspended for several days without pay. Within a few days, both the Commandant and the Sergeant (nicknamed 'Lanky') left the camp altogether. *'Good riddance'*, Round wrote on 13 July 1943. Their departure coincided with the arrival of the new Commandant—known among internees as the 'Pumpkin Controller'—under whom conditions improved slightly.

Equally harsh treatment was meted out to Sye Foo Bok, a young British–Chinese Records Clerk, a few months later. Summoned to the Camp Office on 14 October 1943, his 'offence' was the discovery of a letter he had written to a woman internee—communication between men and women being strictly prohibited. Bok's wife, Rosalind, had given birth to their daughter, Susan Ann, during captivity in August 1942, underscoring the profound personal strain under which he was already living. Determined to extract a confession, the Commandant subjected Bok to prolonged mistreatment: he was forced to kneel for hours, beaten repeatedly over three days, kept sitting upright through the night, denied food, and not allowed to sleep. For over twenty-nine hours, he was interrogated, punished, and compelled to admit to writing the letter.

The authorities treated Bok's case as exemplary. Captain Harold Stratford was instructed to compile a list of all internees who had committed comparable transgressions—those who communicated with women, those who gambled, those who did not smoke but received cigarettes, and all those who bartered cigarettes. If the list was not submitted, the guards warned that cigarettes and hot baths would be withdrawn for a month as collective punishment.

Such displays of cruelty extended beyond the internees themselves. On 24 July 1945, Round noted that *'A Japanese from outside was caught stealing vegetables from the garden by the guards. Whether it was a man or woman—hard to say but the guards thrashed the culprit with sticks making the unfortunate one shriek with pain. It just goes to show that the people outside must be feeling the hunger pangs like ourselves.'* An earlier entry from 7 October 1943 records another disturbing episode: two guards beat a small puppy to death with stones and a hooked pole, reportedly laughing as they did so.

Sporadic acts of violence against men, women, and children accumulated over the months and years of imprisonment, gradually producing an atmosphere in which criminality felt omnipresent. This was precisely the point made by the women in the camp in their letter to the Red Cross[3] in March 1944, where they cited multiple instances of victimisation and appealed for intervention and the restoration of basic human rights:

> We should be most grateful if something could be done to improve our conditions here as at the moment we are treated not as civilian internees but as criminal prisoners. We should like to be treated as adult human beings, to be given freedom of movement within the limits of this building and grounds—and above all to be relieved of the constant nerve strain under which we live as a result of numerous petty regulations numbering 133, a copy of which is attached and which serve no useful purpose but only make our lives unbearable.

Recounting episodes of disgraceful treatment by the guards, the letter highlighted the guards' policy of 'hit at will', which they exercised without restraint. The merciless assault on Mrs. Thoms was one such instance, another demonstrated both the guards' persistence and the complete lack of control exercised by the camp's superior officers.

> Another woman was hit sharply on the head with a key for closing a dining room window. She went immediately to the Office to lodge a complaint—the guard followed her and in front of the Captain slapped her face. Becoming more and more enraged he followed her out of the office,

---

[3] Imperial War Museum, London. Misc 155 Item 2415.

grabbed her by the throat, beat her back across a table preparing to hitting her again. He was however, pulled off by the interpreter, whereupon he seized a chair and went for her.

The sheer malice in these actions is almost unimaginable. Even children were not spared. On one occasion, a ten-year-old boy, returning from the refuse pit after emptying a bin, paused to make snowballs. As punishment he was made to stand for an hour and a half in pouring sleet on a bitterly cold day. No one was allowed to give him a coat, and his clothes were soon soaked through. He developed a chill, followed shortly by jaundice. Medical attention was scant, and when requested, granted very reluctantly. Denial of food for the sick was standard, and the so-called 'special diet' amounted to no more than a cup of soup. The guards' insensitivity is evident from another occasion, where milk prescribed for a child patient was taken away and given instead to a dog belonging to the camp authorities.

The most inhuman instance of child abuse is documented in a report dated December 1942, signed by the mothers of the children 'accused'— Madeline Charnaud, Helen Guy, and Ethel Marion Spark. Madeline's son Michael was 11, Helen's son Howard only 7, and Marion's son Graham 10. Their 'offence' was breaking a pane in a glass door while playing with a ball. Summoned to the Camp Office for interrogation, the boys were found by their mother in a state of terror— weeping and trembling, their upper clothing removed, while two pokers were being heated on the fire, apparently in preparation for branding as punishment. The mothers were held responsible. When Mrs. Charnaud pleaded for leniency, noting that the children had already suffered greatly, Captain Wimoto retaliated by ordering the mothers to remove the pokers from the brazier and 'brand' their own children. They broke down and refused, whereupon the

Captain terrified the boys further and proceeded to singe their hair with the heated poker. The interpreter, Midori Kawa, was equally malicious, treating the brutality as a source of sadistic amusement. Michael Charnaud speaks of this horrific incident in the BBC series 'A Child's War–Part 10':

> Captain Stratford very quietly and firmly told the Commandant and the Interpreter, who had been enjoying the torment and egging him on, that if any child was touched or in any way harmed, the two of them would be reported to the War Crimes tribunal after the War and they could face the most serious punishment with possible execution for attacking and molesting children which in the West was considered a Capital Crime.[4]

As for the boys, their psyche was to be indelibly branded by this incident. Witnesses to a series of such traumatic incidents, each POW in the camp drew upon whatever resources he/she could muster to withstand the relentless psychological assault. None emerged unscathed. Suhasini bore her own mental wounds, yet sought to frame this period as a challenging test of spiritual resilience. In her copy of the *Gitanjali*, she wrote in Bengali: '*Nothing here can actually upset me if I try to fill up my mind with all the lovely moments of the past. I spend a lot of my time immersed in my own world*'.

Suhasini was not an escapist; rather, she tried to help her fellow internees maintain cheerfulness, offering hope in moments of despair and encouraging them to restore their faith in God. Turning to cherished memories served as a vital survival tactic.

---

[4] Michael Charnaud reported in 'A Child's War Part 10' that 'Wimoto, the Commandant, and Sato his Head Guard or assistant and the Interpreter were all sentenced for War Crimes in 1947 and given 5 years, which following pretrial detention was reduced to 3 years and 4 months!'

The cheerful 'Miss Curtis', like several others, attempted to cope with the camp's travails by outwitting the guards and learning to adapt to the harsh circumstances. A verse she composed in the Fukushima Camp (now at the Imperial War Museum), entitled 'If'—an unmistakable allusion to Kipling's famous 1895 poem—encapsulates this strategy of endurance and survival.

> If you can laugh at things you find distressing,
> And after months of waiting still have hope,
> If you can wash yourself without undressing,
> And quite forget about that thing called soap,
> If you can smile and 'keyrie' (to bow) most politely,
> To Japs while cursing them within your heart,
> If you can rise at six each morning brightly,
> And clean a 'Bengo' (lavatory) for a happy start
> If you can stuff with bread until it kills you,
> As the septic tank has proved to be revealing —
> If you can starve on food that never fills you
> And miss no opportunity of stealing,
> If you can turn away from men discreetly,
> And never talk to them before a guard
> If behind his back you break the rule completely,
> And smile and wave at them across the yard.
> If you can heed each optimistic rumour,
> And feel next month must surely be the last
> If you can always keep a sense of humour,
> And plan the future, not regret the past.
> If you can learn to be a cunning schemer
> And never miss a chance to have some fun,
> You'll find life, not so bad in Fukushima,
> And can be sometimes quite a happy one.

6

Survival Strategies

Unsurprisingly, the harshly regimented life in the internment camp life left its scars on the inmates' psyche. In the early days of internment, false hope was constantly sustained by the prospect of an impending exchange of prisoners. On 30 September 1942, a few months after they had been taken prisoner, the Commandant spoke of 'hopes of release soon'. Yet, release remained an elusive dream, mentioned only from time to time. In his diary entry dated 2 September 1943, Fox notes, *'The Commandant told the Greek Captain that we would leave on the first exchange ship'*. This assurance proved to be a mirage, and life in the camp went on, with the internees—individually and collectively—trying to figure out strategies to hold their minds and spirits together.

As the days and months of confinement continued, there was an increasing infringement on individual freedom and rights. On 7 November 1942, ten men and a few women were allowed to write letters to their relatives—letters that, in all likelihood, were never posted, since the camp's existence remained a secret. For several months, all writing material and books, as well as communication with the outside world through letters, newspapers, and radio, had been banned. A diary entry by Fox for 29 February 1944 records that after months of deprivation, internees *'have been informed that we can write home. Paper and other material tomorrow'*. Another diary entry by Round notes that a prisoner was allowed to write one hundred words home once a month, and one could only write about health. Censorship was clearly in place. On 1 March 1944, the Passenger Superintendent of the managing agents of The Eastern and Australian Steamship Company privately circulated a '*copy of letters addressed to relatives by prisoners of war in Japan ex Nankin*'. The content of these letters, when compared with testimonies recorded in personal diaries, reveals the extent of Japanese surveillance and censorship. Each letter reassures family members that the writer is '*in good health*', '*extremely fit*', and '*in the best of spirits*', leaving no cause for worry. The discrepancy between these public records and the private observations of camp life is only too apparent.

As late as August 1944, Suhasini's sister Surama sent communication through the Red Cross Society in Tokyo, Japan, which read thus:

> All well. Mother anxious for news. Letters written but no reply. Bultu's boy one year old. School working. Friends well. Jess, Edna returned. Keep cheerful. S. Biswas.

THE EASTERN AND AUSTRALIAN STEAMSHIP CO. LTD.
(INCORPORATED IN ENGLAND)

MACDONALD, HAMILTON & CO., MANAGING AGENTS

UNION HOUSE, 247 GEORGE STREET

SYDNEY

TELEGRAPHIC AND CABLE ADDRESS
" NALDHAM "

BOX No. 545X, G.P.O.
PHONE B 7611 (6 LINES)

PASSENGER SUPERINTENDENT.   1st March,   194 4.

                    CIRCULAR.   For private circulation only and
                                           none of the news contained herein
                                           should be given to any newspaper
                                           or other publication.

Dear Sir/Madam,

        Since we wrote to you on the 16th September last, the
following copy of letters addressed to relatives by prisoners
of war in Japan ex "Nankin" have been received by us:-

Copy of letter addressed by Mr.H.R.Conn, 3rd Engineer, to his
Mother, from No. 1 Camp, Tokyo Area, dated 10/3/43.
"   I am in good health and being well treated also have plenty
of clothes so do not worry. Hope you, Dad and all are well.
Never heard if I have another niece or nephew. The allotment
still carries on, carry on as before, take what you want -
trouble of any kind see Union. Regards to relatives and
friends, ask all to write. Christmas Day spent pleasantly.
See Red Cross about writing and anything you wish to send.
Look after yourselves, never worry. Keep your chin up, mine
is. Longing to see you all. Cheerio for the present. Love".

Copy of letter sent by Mr. B.W.Dun, Chief Officer, to his Wife,
dated 10/3/43.

"   First letter can only write one letter so pass around. Am
well and cheerful Hope all are well. Christmas Day received
Red Cross food parcel very welcome. Hope more follow. Send
through Red Cross plus 1 set Scholes Anterior Metatarsal Arch
supports size 8 Heavy Duty, also 3 sets spare leathers and
rivets for same. Lost all snaps. Please send some - tell
Bonnie Brae's folk same. Give all home news. Hope Hilda doing
well at school. Robert growing big and talking now I expect.
When did you receive news of me? Hope allotment O.K."

Copy of letter addressed by Mr.F.W.Harris, 2nd Steward, to his
Parents, from No. 1 Prison Camp, Tokyo Area, dated 6/3/43.

"   I am extremely fit and well and in excellent spirit, so
please do not worry about me. We had a very good Christmas,
each receiving a Red Cross parcel packed with foodstuffs, they
were very much appreciated. I will have lots of stories to

                            2.

tell you when we arrive home. Each and every day I think of you
all and hope that you will not have changed. I even have a
holiday trip for us planned. Do not forget that if ever you or
Auntie Alice are short of money that I would like you to use mine,
also try to keep the car running; continue to draw my money.
Write telling me how you are. Lots of love".

Copy of letter addressed by Mr.R.B.Shepherd, 6th Engineer, to his
Parents, from No. 1 Prison Camp, Tokyo Area, dated 9/3/43.

"   Have had no letters yet, but I think of home continually, and
trust you and Dad are O.K. and well, also Lindesay, Russell, Rene,
Baby and Judith. Please do not worry Mum, am in good health and
spirits, hoping to be with you all again in the not far distant
future. Regards to the whole family, Pat and friends.

        I wish Ross and Len best of luck. Regards to the Surf Club
chaps. Hope to get letters soon with photos of family. I have
good clothes and stood winter well. Got Red Cross parcel for
Christmas. Hope Russell remains home. My love to the little
fellow".

The copy of letters circulated by the Passenger Superintendent

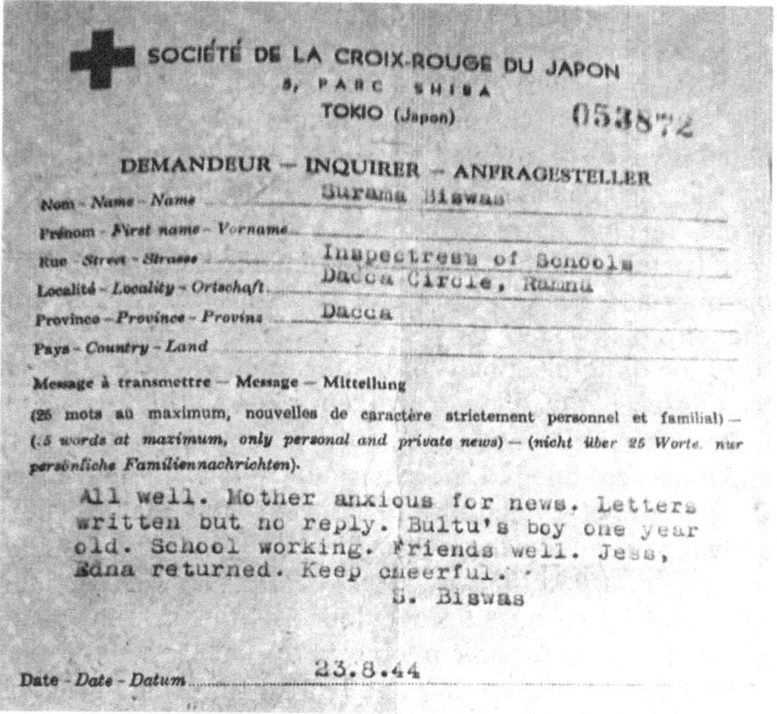

Surama's correspondence with Suhasini via the Red Cross Society in Japan

Writing letters to loved ones back home was an activity that kept the prisoners' minds occupied; waiting for and receiving letters was an even more significant event that lifted their spirits and briefly effaced the dreary monotony of camp life. When the first letters began arriving after months of total communication blackout, there was a sense of collective joy and sharing. This explains two entries for 5 and 18 March 1945 recorded by Round: '*Miss Biswas received a cable from India*'. In one of the pages of Suhasini's exercise book are several dates, all after March 1944, which list her correspondents—her sister (N'di), Miss Edna Hale, her brother (Khoka), her mother, her elder brother

(Dada), her Mejdi, and the Director of Public Instruction, who was in charge of her employment. The 'once a month' concession to write letters was meticulously observed, and over the months Suhasini sought to ease anxieties at home by asserting that '*I can keep myself fit and cheerful*', even as she confessed her own longing to hear tidings from home, receive news of her mother, and stay connected with friends. Her letters mention remembering each family member and friend during the daily services in the camp chapel.

While long-distance communication with family and friends was obviously restricted, even within the camp interaction between men and women—even husbands and wives confined in the same camp—was not permitted. On 29 October 1943, more than a year after the prisoners' arrival at the Fukushima camp, Fox notes: '*Husbands and wives met for first time in Assembly Hall. They had 1½ hours together.*' Later, on 14 November 1943, they were again allowed to meet for half an hour in the garden.

The pain of separation and the strain of being unable to envision the future led to a psychological state in which many internees turned to the past. Dreams evoking memories of happier times became one means of survival during these traumatic days. In November 1943, Suhasini speaks of a night when she could not sleep because she was hungry, as they had not been served dinner. She writes: '*Paul's Epistle a real help at this time. Dreamt of Sejdi having a baby. Na'di looking so pretty and slim.*' Similarly, on 27 August 1943, Fox writes: '*Dreamt about folks at home...*' With little to distinguish one day from another, many internees marked the passage of time by recalling anniversaries and birthdays. On 25 October 1942, Fox notes in his diary: '*My wedding anniversary. I spent the day by having my weekly hot bath and receiving a set of winter underclothing from the Japs. Blankets issued today—felt intense cold for over a week.'* On the same day, the following year (1943) he writes, '*Second wedding anniversary celebrated by mending "Nanking Road". For second time went to church.*'

The chapel and Christian religious services were indeed a source of spiritual sustenance for the faithful. Suhasini quotes from *Isaiah 55* and reiterates her devotion: '*We will come and make our abode with him*'. Yet at times differences arose concerning church services, and Suhasini tried to maintain a balance between the groups within the context of their collective life in the camp. In the middle of January 1945, she writes in her notebook,

> Everything considered and with all due respect to the genuine religious convictions represented in the camp, we believe it would be fair to all concerned if we took half of the evenings available and if you took the other half preferably taking alternative months thus avoiding unnecessary controversy encouraging a positive delivery of our respective messages.

During the Christmas season in the winter of 1943, choir practice for a special church service scheduled for Christmas Eve sparked great enthusiasm among the internees. A radio was installed on 24 March 1944, and connection with the outside world was re-established. Within the camp, these developments followed quickly on the heels of the International Red Cross discovering the Fukushima internment camp and sending in supplies of food and other daily necessities. After months in oblivion, the civilian internees had finally been detected by an international organisation.

The Camp Rules prohibited the playing of musical instruments or the gramophone without permission, as well as singing in the corridors in general and patriotic songs in particular. Only after March 1944 were internees allowed to use the Assembly Hall for music or as a common room. In this context, it is worth recalling that Suhasini must have found deep solace in Tagore's *Gitanjali*, which she had managed to smuggle into the camp. The well-thumbed pages of the book clearly suggest how deeply she absorbed the spirituality of its songs, perhaps experiencing an almost living communion with the divine through the verses where she had left her marginal notes. She must have also sung hymns in the church chapel, where prisoners were allowed to pray on Sundays and during Easter or Christmas. One of the more curious entries appears on the flyleaf of Suhasini's *Gitanjali*, where she had written a very popular Bengali patriotic song by the poet Dwijendralal Ray (*dhana dhanya puspa bhora, amader ei basundhara*).

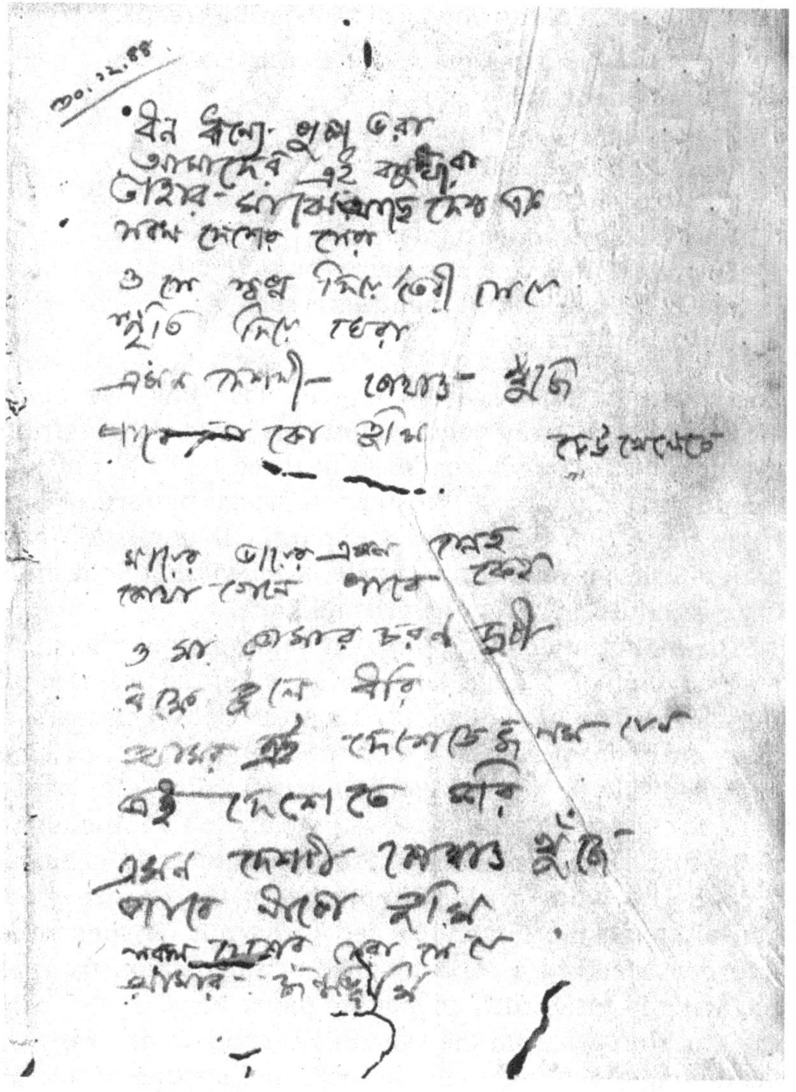

Roy's poem scribbled by Suhasini on Gitanjali's fly leaf

The first stanza of the poem (in translation) reads:

> Flowing with riches, grains and flowers,
> This Mother Earth of ours,
> Amidst her is a country
> Most cherished country of all,
> A country made of dreams
> Encircled by cherished memories,
> Such a country, you may search for but not find anywhere
> She is the queen of all countries is she,
> O my motherland.

Composed in the raga Kedar, the last line, *'se amar janmabhumi'* ('O my motherland'), is used as a refrain throughout the poem, rendered in three types of musical tempo that imitate a Western musical pattern. From these notes and entries, it is apparent that religion and nationalism played a crucial role in alleviating Suhasini's distress, infusing her with faith and hope.

The monotony of camp life was reinforced by the strict enforcement of a daily routine, an essential element of the mechanism of control. On 16 April 1943, Fox made a diary entry: *'forced to sign paper for work.'* On 19 April, he recorded that he started work on paper cutting for paper bags, for which he received 1.92 yen; and on 21 August he notes that he had finished work on 29 bundles. Mechanical though the work was, it kept the prisoners occupied, and although the money earned could not be spent, the internees derived a certain sense of satisfaction from it. Engaging in tasks such as making paper bags, ingeniously crafting slippers from the available cardboard and rags, or fashioning functional bamboo forks and spoons served as an outlet for their creative energies.

The children in the camp attended classes conducted by the internees themselves, engaging in activities that resembled those of a regular school. This simulated sense of normalcy not only benefited the children but also kept several of the elders in the camp—many of them teachers by profession—meaningfully occupied.

The idea of organising lessons for the children was first proposed by one of the prisoners, David Millar, Second Mate of the *SS Willesden*, after its capture by the Germans. He devised the plan following his encounter with the new prisoners from the *SS Nankin* aboard the *Regensberg*. Millar had befriended two young boys, Howard Gunstone and Michael Charnaud, aged six and eleven at the time. They were intrigued as they watched Millar measuring shadows on the ship's deck to calculate their position in mid-ocean in the absence of any map. Their curiosity prompted Millar to volunteer to teach them mathematics to help them keep up with their schoolwork. This required asking the Germans for permission to start classes and trick them into providing pencil and paper. It was in this context that Madeline Charnaud mentioned a co-passenger from the *Nankin*: '*a Miss Biswas, [is] a schoolteacher, and we've already spoken to her about starting up classes for the children. If you were to teach them mathematics I'm sure it would fit in splendidly*'.[1] In *Lost at Sea, Found at Fukushima*, Andy Millar chronicles his father David's experience as a POW and notes that Millar soon spoke to Suhasini, described as '*a middle-aged British Indian woman*', who readily agreed to set up separate classes for the two boys on account of the difference in their ages.

Suhasini's slim, much-thumbed exercise book—which contains diary-like entries, lists of provisions, desultory notes, inspiring quotations, knitting patterns, and a potpourri of scribblings—also includes an assortment of math exercises, perhaps set for the children. On the inside cover of the notebook, written in red pencil—usually reserved for school corrections—are the words 'School Notes'.

---

[1] Madeline Charnaud has been quoted in Millar's book on p.86.

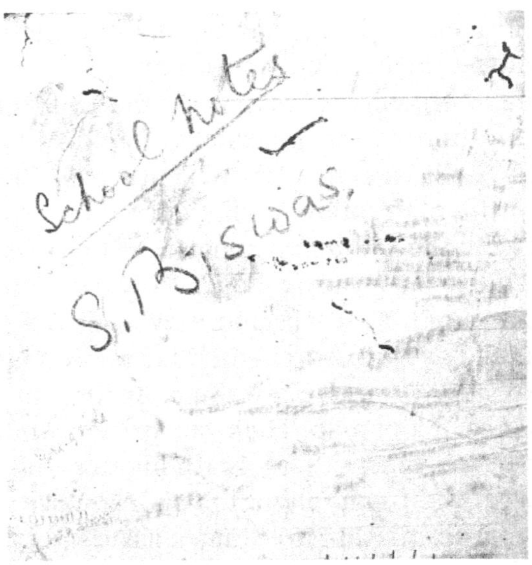

The inside cover of Suhasini's notebook

The two pupils were issued report cards titled 'Fukushima Tutorials' similar to formal school term reports, complete with examination scores, teacher's comments, and signatures.[2] The entire arrangement was carried out with utmost seriousness. When Michael Charnaud turned twelve on 31 March 1943, he and Graham Sparkes were transferred to the men's section, where David Millar and Alfie Round conducted longer and more engaging teaching sessions with them. The boys were allowed to visit their mothers in the women's section every day, and Madeleine Charnaud continued to give them geography lessons. The older boys were introduced to a range of games, activities, and interests that kept the male internees occupied, and they welcomed the change. Meanwhile, little Howard, who continued to live in the women's quarters, missed his playmates.

---

[2] Andy Millar reproduces Charnaud's report card in *Lost at Sea Found at Fukushima: The Story of a Japanese POW* on p.169.

Through such efforts, the prisoners sought to create a healthy, 'normal' community that, despite ego clashes and differences, held the diverse group together throughout their period of incarceration. Suhasini observes in her exercise book how *'Language is a barrier but at times a great use specially when cannot be interpreted. Humour keeps us alive. Oh! for a real sense of it. Going to be better is the idea that pulls us thro[ugh].'*

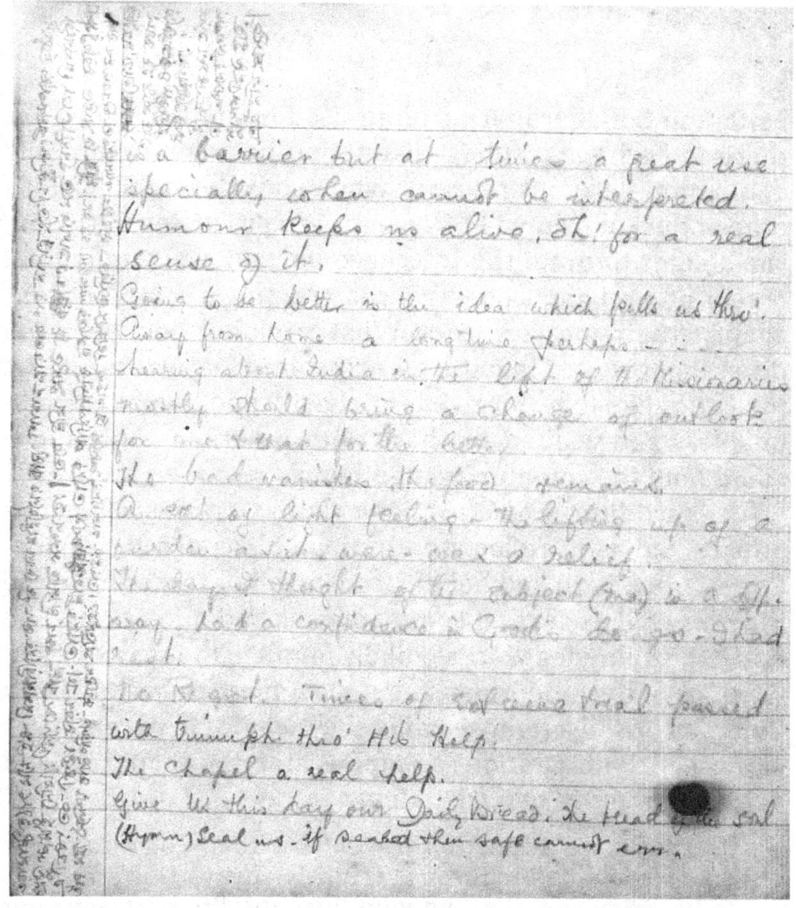

Suhasini's exercise book with the quoted lines

7

Faith and Belief

Faith and belief are terms often used interchangeably, yet there is perhaps a subtle distinction between them. This distinction becomes relevant when considering Suhasini's time at the Fukushima POW camp. As a practising Christian, she sought to unite the internees beyond their individual creeds and religious observances, creating a common front against their incarcerators. What troubled her were the differences rooted in faith; what inspired her was the belief in virtues like love, forgiveness, charity and humaneness—qualities she wanted to share with others, as only these could hold the community together.

In her slim exercise book with its miscellaneous entries, Suhasini reflects on various ideas about religion, Christianity, faith and belief, drawing on passages from the Bible as well as several commentaries and quotations. She notes the following words—likely found in the sermons and writings of the modernist, anti-race American pastor Harry Emerson Fosdick (whose name she includes in parentheses alongside the quotation)—emphasising the empirical and practical practice of Christianity:

> If religion be a function by which either God's cause or man's cause (which if it is truth is always God's also) is to be advanced, then he who lives the life of it however

narrowly is a better servant than he who merely knows about it.

For Suhasini, practising the Christian values of patience and tolerance, truth and obedience, love and suffering, constituted the essence of her religion. She notes, '*As before we shall meet as members of Christ in this locality in other words as in Christ at Fuku [shima] and we believe that all who are cleansed by Christ's blood and baptised by his spirit into the one body (Cor. 12.12) should take the opportunity to gather regularly in His name according to Acts 2.42–47, of Heb 10.5, Luke 22.19.*'

Across the internees at Fukushima, Christianity—with its denominational diversity and internal differences—was probably the single largest faith in the camp. There were Catholics, Protestants, Baptists and members of the Greek Orthodox Church—all professing faith in Christ but differing in doctrinal practices and beliefs. The Greeks in the camp tended to keep aloof during religious occasions. In an entirely different socioeconomic context, the thinker and philosopher Karl Marx had called religion the 'opium of the people'. Classical social theorists like Karl Marx, W. E. B. Du Bois and Max Weber argued that the disenfranchised and suffering often found more comfort in religion and in maintaining the status quo than in protest or revolution, which might realistically bring about dramatic change. In the POW camp, under conditions of incarceration where the Japanese authorities exercised strict control, power and surveillance, the possibility of any collective uprising to demand freedom was out of the question. Religious faith thus functioned as a psychological and spiritual 'opiate', a resource that sustained a sense of wellbeing essential to enduring experiences of suffering. In Suhasini's entry dated 10 June 1944, she writes,

For many weeks the Lord has been burdening us for the spiritual needs of those in this place, and the prayers of our hearts has been heard. "Point out the weights that are hindering Lord." We do believe that He in a measure answered this prayer last week and showed us that if we really desired His best we should as far as possible seek to comply with the regulations here. We gladly and willingly obeyed His revealed will and even if he lays further claims upon us, I think that we can all say that we shall willingly follow His leading regardless of the cost. Ever since the Lord led you to take the studies in Timothy of Titus, He has shown us clearly that it is impossible for us to expect His unhindered blessing if we are not absolutely faithful to His word regarding false teaching. We are sure that if you read the following passages carefully and prayerfully again in Scofield's Bible He will give you further Revelation.

Needless to say we have prayed very much over this letter. We know that you are as eager for God's glory in this place as we are and we know that if you prayerfully lay this matter before Him without reservation depending absolutely on His spirit for guidance, He will reveal to you it is perfect Will (John 7:17). Our object in writing instead of speaking is that we feel that you can more quietly and prayerfully consider this all-important question with the help of God's word. Later on when you feel free, we shall be happy to know what the God had been saying to you.

It becomes obvious that Suhasini represented a group in the camp who handled the exigencies of everyday life by depending on their absolute faith in the will of Christ, believing that accepting their divinely ordained destiny was the lesson in obedience expected of a good Christian.

On 8 July 1945, Round writes in his diary that the sirens had gone off frequently during the previous night and early morning, leading him to suspect that *the Yanks must have been coming over in waves...*'. Hope grounded in faith sustains him in the unbearable conditions, and he looks towards the future: '*Only God knows of the joy which awaits us all when we leave this distressing and spirit breaking prison camp. The whole place can be summed up in two words (Concentrated evil)*'.

Continuing with this train of thought in an entry two days later, on 10 July, Round writes of the *'Great troubles'* he was facing personally that have,

> ...[t]aken me completely off my feet. Only God knows the depths of it and only He can help me. Praise his Holy name. Still the great rejection goes on. Men in the camp as well as the women refuse to come to Christ, our blessed Lord and Saviour. Night and day nothing but blasphemies and evil speaking goes on.

A sense of abjection seemed to pervade several internees. Yet, each sought to preserve his/her spiritual and emotional well-being, holding on to faith as a means of maintaining sanity. For some, this took the form of an unquestioning belief in a moral universe where wrong-doers would ultimately face punishment. On 21 July 1945, Round's diary entry reads:

> The very elements are warring against Japan. The rice crops seem to be in a bad state as it has been raining continually for a week... The valley is shrouded with low lying clouds. The whole place is one picture of misery and despair. It gives one the feeling that we are surrounded by countless members of the powers of darkness. How wonderful to know that in the midst of our trials and perplexities, Christ the prince of light stands by our side and succours us. As I write now I feel as if I am in the Devil's very clutches; all joy seems to have left me. But I know that the trial of our faith is precious in the Father's sight... May God enable us to speak plenty of words fitting for our Lord Jesus.

Several of the internees, including Suhasini, who possessed a deep and institutionalised faith, found in religion a pillar of strength—one that offered them both hope and courage amid the darkness of despair. For Suhasini, in addition to Christianity, the songs of Tagore's *Gitanjali* offered immense emotional sustenance. Inspired by Song 7, with the date '29 April'43' entered close to the opening line, the marginalia at the bottom of the page appears to be dovetailed with an entry from a later year and time. The first entry expresses a dedicated faith in the divine and a steady conviction that 'His Will' will be fulfilled. It takes the shape of a prayer: '*Show, show your light; so many dreams, going to them again and again, those in trouble will see them end.*'

The second entry, undated, refers to 15 April, the Bengali New Year, when '*past memories come flooding in*'. Yet it also records a bleak present: a sudden drop in rationed bread, the lowering of morale among camp mates, and the persistent pangs of hunger. Strains of the song offer spiritual sustenance:

> Enter my life in ever-new forms,
> Come as fragrance and colour, appear as music,
> Come to my body as thrilling touch,
> Come to my soul as joyous delight,
> Come to my vision, subliminal and inward-looking,
> Come as beauty, calm and tranquil,
> Come ruled by mysterious strangeness,
> Come in sorrow and joy, entering my conscious mind,
> Come each day in all I do,
> Come at the closure of all my work. (Tagore 2023)

8

Song and Consolation

The British war poet, Wilfred Owen (1893–1918), who died a week before the Armistice (11 November 1918), is known to have read and admired the poems of Rabindranath Tagore, compiled in *Gitanjali: Song Offerings*. It was a slim volume of 103 poems, translated from the original Bengali into English poetic prose by the poet, the first non-European Nobel Laureate for Literature. The poems were introduced to European/English-reading audiences by William Rothenstein and William Butler Yeats in 1912.[1] In the introduction, Yeats wrote of the mesmerising impact of the poems on him:

> I have carried the manuscript of these translations about with me for days, reading it in railway trains, or on the top of omnibuses and in restaurants, and I have often had to close it lest some stranger would see how much it moved me. These lyrics—which are in the original, my Indian friends tell me, full of subtlety of rhythm, of untranslatable delicacies of colour, of metrical invention—display in their thought a world I have dreamed of all my life long. The work of a supreme culture, they yet appear as much the growth of the common soil as the grass and the

---

[1] The Bengali version of *Gitanjali* published in 1910 had 157 songs. Only 50 songs from here were included in the English version. The rest, that is 53 poems, were collected from several other works of the poet.

rushes. A tradition where poetry and religion are the same thing, has passed through the centuries, gathering from learned and unlearned metaphor and emotion, and carried back against the multitude the thought of the scholar and of the noble. (Tagore 1977, xi–xii)

The *Gitanjali* at the time of its international debut, had 'with its vital faith in the redeeming powers of the spiritual forces and their upbuilding energy' (Radhakrishnan 1919, 2), proclaimed 'in no uncertain tones, the utter bankruptcy of materialism' (ibid.). The First World War was imminent, the civilised world was experiencing a crisis in which pride and hate, 'lust for gold and greed of land' (ibid.) became major human and national preoccupations. As Radhakrishnan points out, in the realm of the soul and spirit, there is neither East nor West; rather Rabindranath's work 'meets a general want and satisfies a universal demand' (ibid., Preface).

A few years after Wilfred Owen's death, Susan H. Owen, his mother, wrote a touching letter to 'Sir Rabindranath' from their family home on Monkmoor Road in Shrewsbury, UK, on 1 August 1920.

> It is nearly two years ago, that my dear eldest son, went out to the war for the last time and the day he said goodbye to me—we were looking together across the sun glorified sea, looking towards France with breaking hearts—when he, my poet son, said those wonderful words of yours— beginning at "when I go from hence let this be my last word that what I have seen is unsurpassable... and if the end comes here let it come—let this be my parting word." And when his pocket book came back to me—I found these words written in his clear, writing—with your name beneath—would it be asking too much of you, to tell me what book I should find the whole poem in?[2]

There were raging controversies and misunderstandings in Europe regarding the philosophy of life embedded in

---

[2] This letter is preserved in the Rabindra Bhavana Archives in Santiniketan.

Tagore's poetry. The poet himself believed he was drawing on ancient Indian wisdom, the teachings of the Buddha and the Upanishads. This was vehemently contradicted by a group who argued that he was borrowing from Christianity and, without calling himself a Christian, offering a glimpse of what Christianity might become in India. Tagore did not preach a religion; he did not represent any cult, nor did he formulate any systematic philosophy. 'But we feel that the atmosphere is charged with a particular vision of reality. In his writings we have the reactions of his soul to the environment, his attitude in the face of life' (Radhakrishnan 1919, 7). It was certainly not religion but a shared poetic consciousness of the finite and infinite that drew Wilfred Owen to Tagore's poetry.

The Bengali version of the *Gitanjali*, first published in 1910, differed vastly from the translated version even in its arrangement, selection and number of poems. Suhasini had with her the tenth reprint (1925) of the Bengali book published by the Visva-Bharati publishing department, printed at the Art Press by Nirendranath Mukherjee. It was this imprint that served as her 'Bible' in the camp years. In the 1910 foreword, Tagore notes that some of the first few poems were songs published earlier. His intention was to bring these scattered lyrics together into one collection, recognising a shared affinity of thought that supported their integration with the newly composed poems. The opening poem in the Bengali version is in a song composed in 1906 and first published in *Bangadarshan*, the literary journal founded by Bankim Chandra Chattopadhyay in 1872, which had gone into hibernation before its revival under the Tagore's editorship in 1901. The song expresses utter surrender of ego and self-pride to the divine:

Amar matha nato kore dao he tomar chorondhular tole
Shokol ahankar he amar dubao chokher jole
Bow my head down to the dust at your feet;

Drown all my pride in tears, oh lord. (Tagore 2023, 63)

Carefully underlined in pencil by Suhasini are these lines, with the name of the camp, *Fukushima*, written beside them in Bengali. Rather than a gesture of surrender to the authorities, this was an appeal to relinquish one's ego to the divine—a conviction that proved essential for survival in the harshest conditions.

In the space below on the same page is a paragraph dated 1 April 1943, a brief account of ten-year-old Graham Sparkes' birthday 'celebration' in the camp. It mentions saving a treat for him, one sweet squirrelled away by someone, and a game of pinning the tail on the donkey—the simple joy of togetherness that marked the occasion in captivity. Suhasini adds that seven-year-old Howard Guy was upset that his own birthday had passed without notice, even as she tried to console him. She nurtured a special fondness for this observant little boy, who had picked up the glass cover of her watch after it fell where the children were playing.

Suhasini appears to have been deeply involved in safeguarding the well-being of innocent children in the camp. She participated wholeheartedly in their daily routines of schoolwork and play, doing what she could to restore a sense of everyday normalcy. The children, in turn, responded with affection to her kindness and concern. Suhasini records how, on her birthday—31 December 1943—camp friends extended their love and companionship in ways she would '*remember till the end of my life.*' After tea and games, eight-year-old Howard Guy gave her a piece of bread with sugar, and others shared a single segment of an orange each. These were precious gifts in a place where even adults often squabbled over meagre food rations. Interestingly, in the blank space above Song 28 of the Bengali *Gitanjali* appears a scribbled drawing by little David, a two-year-old, and perhaps his three-year-old sister Sally, campmates with their parents Herbert and Audrey Cook.

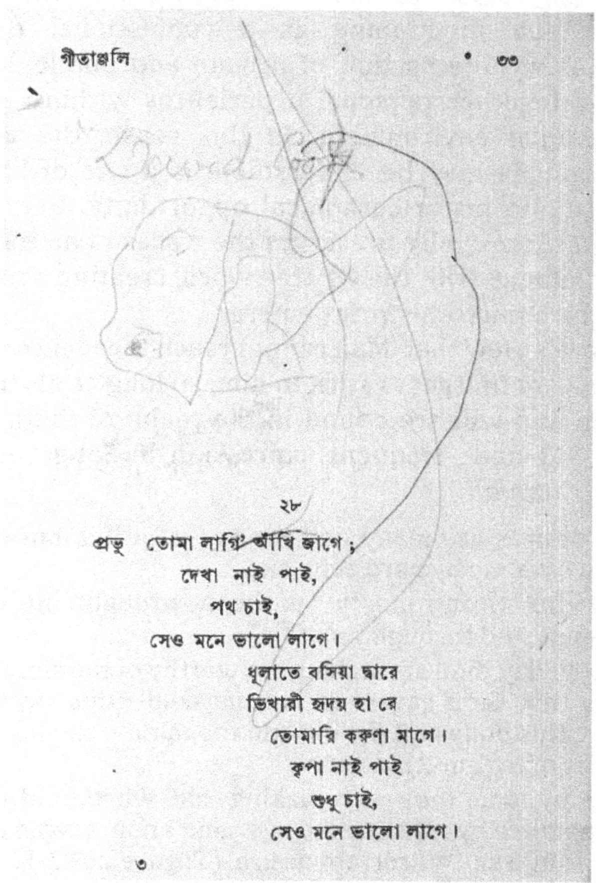

David's drawing above Song 28

The song expresses a wistful longing and hope—the pain of loneliness and loss tempered by a steady faith in divine grace as another New Year approached.

It seems that Suhasini turned to Tagore's songs and poems both to initiate and to reinforce trains of thought that nurtured her conversations with the self, helping her navigate a traumatised psyche struggling under adverse circumstances. The *Gitanjali* became an archive, a dwelling place of memory during her internment. Rather than functioning as a confessional diary, it served as an intersection of private and public domains, bringing together personal experiences within a strange transnational environment. In this sense, the text and its marginalia may be understood as a site of historical evidence and historiographical opportunity. Her copy of *Gitanjali* successfully preserves the traces of an individual life in dialogue with the written word, creating a narrative from which micro-histories emerge.

Tagore's view that 'Man cannot reach the ideal so long as fragments of finiteness stick to him, so long as his intellect, emotion and will are bound in the realm of finite nature' (1919, 34) finds eloquent expression in Song 14[3] of the English *Gitanjali*:

> My desires are many and my cry is pitiful, but ever did thou save me by hard refusals;
> and this strong mercy has been wrought into my life through and through.
> Day by day thou art making me worthy of the simple, great gifts that thou gavest to me unasked—this sky and the light, this body and the life and the mind—saving me from perils of overmuch desire...
> Day by day thou art making me worthy of thy full acceptance by refusing me ever and anon, saving me from perils of weak, uncertain desire. (Tagore 2012, 53)

Camp deprivations—the lack of freedom and the weight of unfulfilled desires—taught one, Suhasini believed, to endure suffering and draw closer to the infinite.

During the internment, birthdays—her own, those of other internees, and even the remembered birthdays of relatives back home—held an ambivalent significance for

---

[3] *Ami bahu basonay pranpone chai/banchita kore banchale more* (Song 2 in the Bengali edition)

her. They were often uncomfortable days of reckoning, when existential uncertainty contended with gratitude for being born and still being alive: '*Why do I feel this strange sense of dejection prior to the birthdays of every loved one... My prayers are to the Almighty*'.

Many birthdays in the camp followed a familiar pattern: waking eagerly to greet the friend warmly, listening to a brief, heartfelt prayer offered by the elderly missionary Annie Law, improvising a makeshift cake from meagre bread rations, and offering tokens of affection—a hanky made from an old piece of cloth or a notebook cobbled together from available slivers of paper.[4]

Yet Suhasini also laments the selfish attitudes that occasionally surfaced within the community and caused hurt, and she longs for the small acts of kindness that could ease the burden of difficult times. It is this triumph of the better self that she finds mirrored in the words on the page.

Amid the mixed racial composition within the camp, Suhasini absorbed the sentiment of the poem—numbered 3 in the Bengali version and 63 in the English *Gitanjali*—which reads:

> Thou hast made me known to friends whom I knew not. Thou hast given me seats in homes not my own. Thou hast brought the distant near and made a brother of the stranger....
>
> Through birth and death, in this world or in others, wherever thou leadest me it is thou, the same, the one companion of my endless life who ever linkest my heart with bonds of joy to the unfamiliar. (Tagore 2012, 203)

Suhasini's entry at the foot of this song refers to a fairly uneventful day—being allowed to sit outside for a while, sharing Urdu lessons with two others, and finishing a small

---

[4] Suhasini's pencilled notes on 4 April 1943, below Song 2 of the Bengali *Gitanjali* record the birthday of Audrey Jeffrey, a young British lady.

handmade gift for Joyce Galsworthy, a British schoolteacher whose husband, a missionary, was also in the camp, though the two were separated under camp rules. Coming so soon after Audrey's birthday, Joyce's own occasion—and the deliberate act of preparing for it—reinforced camp bonds and helped dispel prevailing negativities.

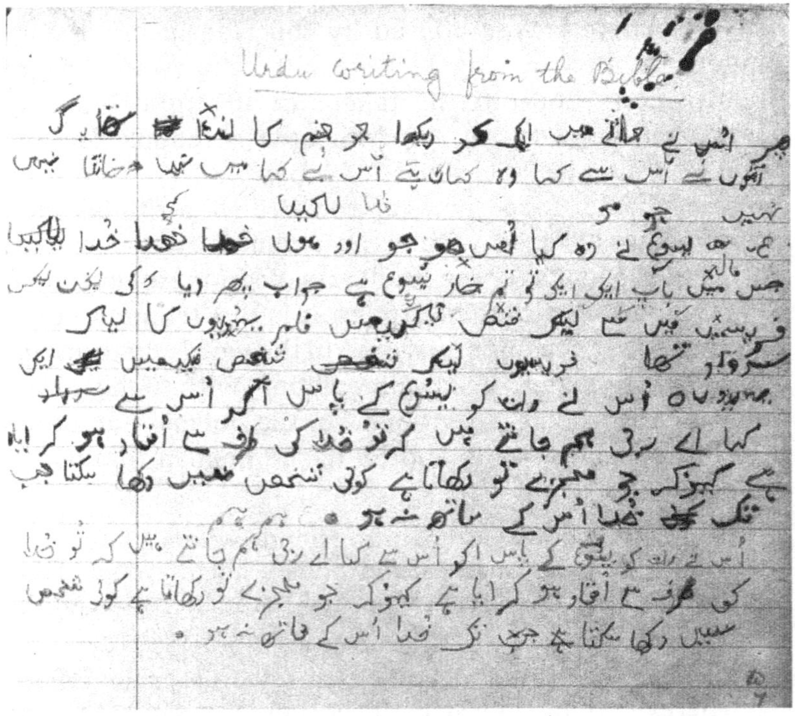

A page from Suhasini's notebook showing her Urdu writing

Suhasini's dialogue with each poem in the *Gitanjali* comes alive through these cryptic pencil entries in Bengali. One such exchange, written beside Song 4 of the Bengali version (*bipade more raksha koro/ e nohe mor prarthana*), translates as a plea to the Almighty for inner strength:

> Protect me from danger is not my prayer,
> Let me not fear danger.
> It will not matter if you deny me solace in sorrow,
> Let me conquer sorrow.
> If none supports me, let my own strength suffice.
> If I suffer worldly loss and am betrayed,
> Let me not lose my inner power.
> That you will save me is not what I pray for,
> Let me have the strength to overcome.
> It will not matter if you do not lighten my burden,
> Let me be able to bear it. (Tagore 2023, 70)

Suhasini writes in the margin in June 1943 that '*in hunger and in thirst I have truly been able to say this*'. At the end of the song is another extended entry, probably referring to the birthday of Monica Lee (a British–Chinese internee) on 8 April, noting how the inmates stole a few moments of joy with Monica that evening when Helen Guy sent them some food to share. Laughter and tears accompanied the prisoners' daily lives, and Suhasini refers to the camp as 'Hell', where small, unpalatable incidents unfolded from daybreak onwards—innumerable tests of patience and tolerance, quarrels that woke her up from sleep at least six times, the camaraderie of the day ironically slipping away.

Trauma, fear and deprivation form a recurring undercurrent in camp life, reflected in the internees' repeated references to violence and hunger, while their survival instinct often finds expression in dreams and memories of freer times. There are also eerie silences discernible in Suhasini's minimalist entries, suggesting the gap between language and lived reality. These shared traumas weave together a narrative that 'constitutes their historical witness' (Caruth 1996, 8), gathering events that testify not only to the unbearable horrors of the airfields and battlefields of the Second World War but also the crises that shaped human survival. One may well ask whether 'the trauma [is] the encounter with death, or the ongoing experience of having survived it?' (ibid., 7).[5]

Suhasini observes that *the ways of human beings are unfathomable* even as she notes moments of respite when the internees could spend time in the garden, continue with their Urdu lessons, or purposefully engage in small crafts such as making little bookmarks as gifts for camp friends[6]— remarks that accompany her comment on the improvement in food that kept spirits afloat. She links these reflections to Song 5 (Bengali) in the *Gitanjali*, seeking an expansive blooming of the soul, an inner resilience expressed through purity and radiance. The lines of the song (*jukto koro he shobar shonge/mukto koro he bandho*) suggest that forming connections with others or with the community loosens restraining bonds, ushering in the joy of awakening to divine glory.

---

[5] In her 1996 book *Unclaimed Experience: Trauma, Narrative and History*, psychoanalyst Cathy Caruth describes this as a 'double telling' that marks an 'oscillation between a crisis of death and the correlative crisis of life' (1996, 7–8).
[6] Suhasini had been gifted in turn a small knife and fork made out of slivers of bamboo by one of the male internees.

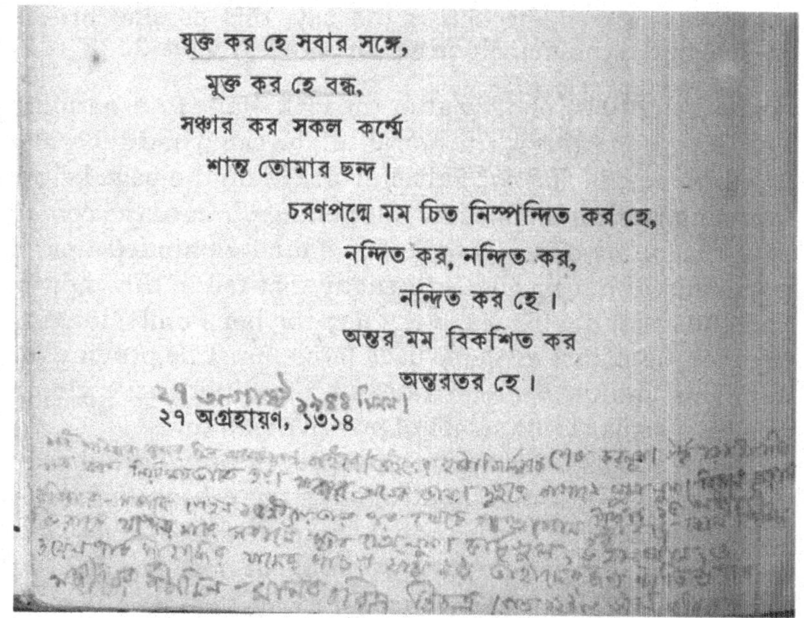

Song 5 of the Gitanjali, with Suhasini's scribblings

The date noted on the page is 27 August 1944, alongside the phrase '*getting together*'. She also records a memorial service in the chapel for the lost seamen of the *Kirkpool*, *Willesden* and *Welpark*. This internalisation of the divine, she suggests, inspires her 'real self' to voluntary acts of selfless kindness and love. Such a state is what Radhakrishnan describes as the 'trans-valuation of all values' (1919, 109).

Despite the persistent pangs of hunger, the irregularity of meals, and the emotional insecurity of anticipating dreaded punishments, Suhasini's awareness of seasonal changes sustained her sense of connection with the divine. In Song 30 of the Bengali version (Song 59 in English; *Ei je tomar prem ogo hriday horono*), she finds her own thoughts echoed in every word written by the poet:

Yes, I know, this is nothing but thy love, O beloved of my heart – this golden light that dances upon the leaves, these idle clouds sailing across the sky, this passing breeze leaving its coolness upon my forehead. (Tagore 2012, 185)

It was April 1944, shortly after the visit of the International Red Cross volunteers. The morale of the camp had generally lifted. '*Beautiful Spring*', Suhasini writes on the page below this song, noting small camp happenings. '*Heard the cooing of a cuckoo at dawn today*'. The sound reminded her of home and of her mother's birthday that fell in this month. She adds that she prays every day for her family, longing to meet them, just as those back home must be praying for her. This ability to discern beauty amid pervasive gloom reveals a remarkable strain of positive thinking.

Below Song 25, during the biting December cold, Suhasini wakes up one morning and remarks on '*a beautiful scene, snow and sunlight.*' Yet her next sentence reads: '*Every day the pangs of hunger are increasing. What does one do? One must bear it. The Lord gives strength.*'

Another April entry from 1943, written in the margins of Song 8 (Bengali; *Aaj dhaner khete roudra chayay*), refers to Easter Sunday and the resurrection of the Lord. Suhasini describes Holy Week—the reading of scripture and the celebrations: '*There was music at night that uplifts the soul... It is the day of resurrection. Everything seems different, there is also similarity. In the Catholic Church a lady decorated it with flowers – without connecting how can the Lord's order be fulfilled.*'

The spirit and rhythm of the song on that page evoke a sense of joy, captured in the play of sunlight and shade on the rural rice fields of Birbhum, a game of hide-and-seek between sun and clouds. Nostalgia blends with a sense of beauty, and as she notes elsewhere about another song, she hummed to herself, '*It is a song for the youth. Joy, joy, joy, with Joy my heart is ringing.*'

Let's not go home today, let's not go home.
We'll break open the skies and loot the world outside.

Like clustering foam in tidal waters,
laughter is bubbling in the wind today.
Playing flutes the whole of today
we shall spend without work. (Tagore 2023, 75)

Rehearsing the *Gitanjali* songs that celebrate the beauty of the physical and cosmic universe brings a deep sense of healing to individual consciousness. The innocent joy of nature invoked by the song filled Suhasini's mind with a quiet satisfaction—an experience of being touched by divine grace. Her documentation of camp life is itself a reflexive act, a form of lived trauma rather than mere narrative recollection. Thus, the sequence of events is interspersed with abrupt phrases: '*Monday, rotten apples...too little food ... listlessness all around ... all the time, my mind is full of old memories, I like spending time in my own world...*'

Consecutive pages in the *Gitanjali* record a series of loosely connected events. On Monday, 26 April, she notes going up to the sentry box at the gate. She recalls a family event—the death, probably of a niece almost 17–20 years ago—situating that old loss against the ever-present uncertainty of camp life with its pervasive threat and constant awareness of mortality. Alluding to everyday meanness, she makes a passing reference to a Mrs Gleason (Loraine Elizabeth Gleason, a merchant seaman and stewardess in her mid-forties) who would later die in the camp in 1945 due to medical complications and lack of treatment. Lines underlined in the Bengali Song 9 (*Anonderi sagar theke esheche aaj baan*) speak of the grit and determination needed to face adversity as a community.

The entry for 28 April presents a glimpse of hope and happiness, for which she thanks God. Yet on 29 April she describes being distraught through the night, her thoughts drifting to a sister back home. '*How I lose control over myself*', she confesses, adding that she misses her mother most of all.

Across these fragmented entries—past memories, current conversations, troubling dreams, episodes of physical discomfort—one encounters a consciousness fractured by trauma yet striving to hold together a sense of meaning.

Suhasini's faith was deep and strong. Yet moments of doubt surfaced from time to time, requiring renewed affirmation of her otherwise firm convictions. Her notings on the Bengali Song 33 (*abar era ghireche mor mon/abar chokhe name aboron*) reveal such moments of internal conflict. The song seeks to ward off troubles and external distractions that pull the mind away from God, the source of all positive force. Unlike other entries, here Suhasini composes her thoughts in two sets of four lines of her own verse, entering into direct dialogue with Tagore's words. The poem describes wavering opinions and the mind's tendency to stray from the shelter of the divine. Suhasini replies:

> How many times do I make mistakes
> How many days is the bond broken
> Can't you bind me tight
> To sit at your feet?

The seeker calls upon the divine for constant protection and guidance, asking for enlightenment. Suhasini writes:

> This earth of yours is a beauty
> Why tarnish it with evil
> Destroy every part of it
> Let your pure arrow fly.

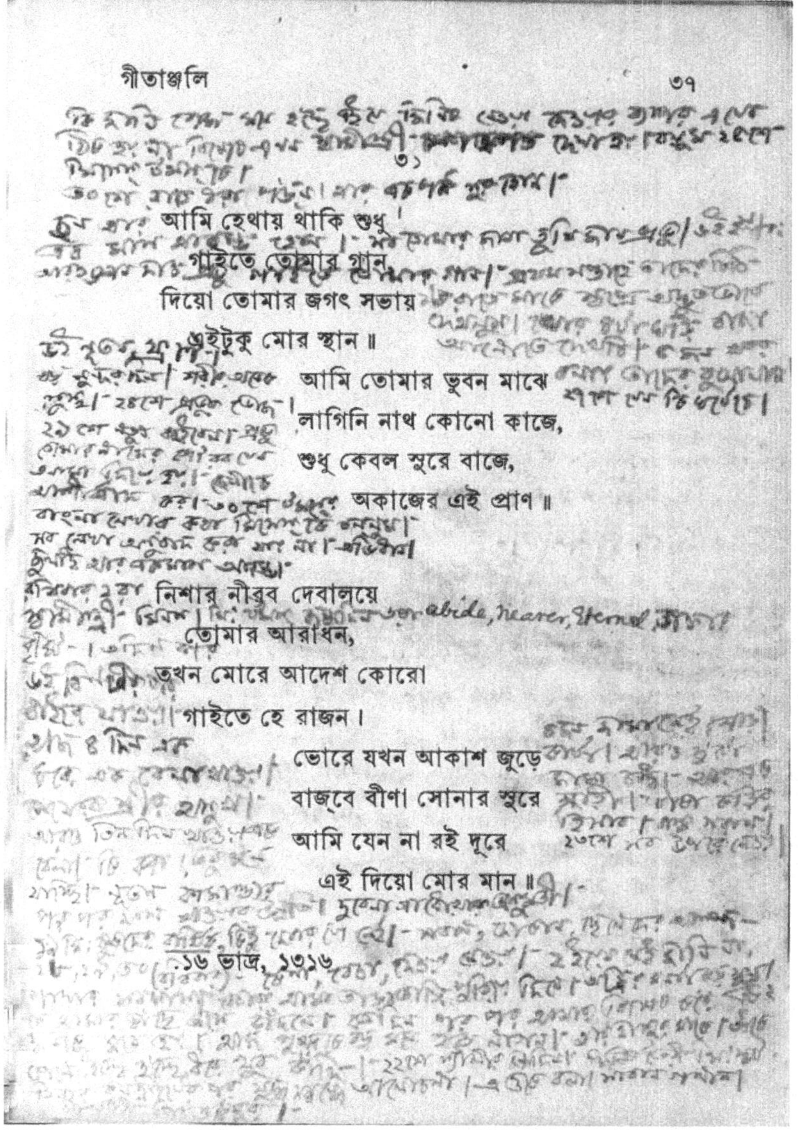

Suhasini's notes along Song 57 where she talks about four consecutive days when they were given only one inadequate meal

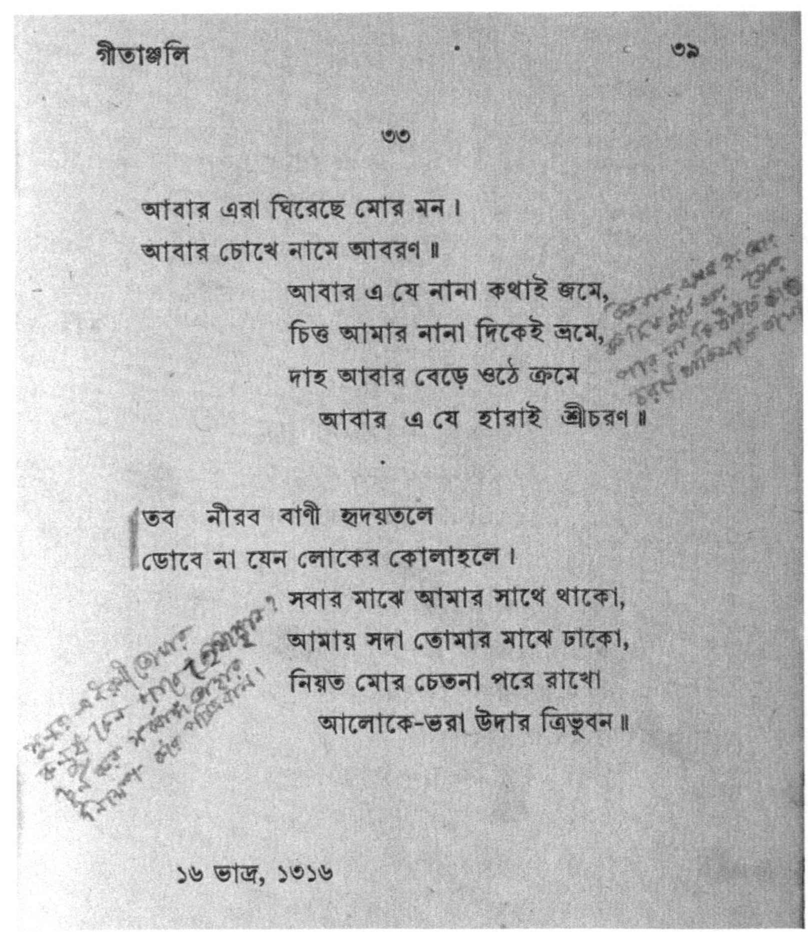

Song 33 with Suhasini's scribblings

Optimism brims over, however, from the final lines of Song 11 (*Tomar shonar thalay sajabo aaj dukher ashrudhar*), which envision the transformation of worries into gold and darkness into light.

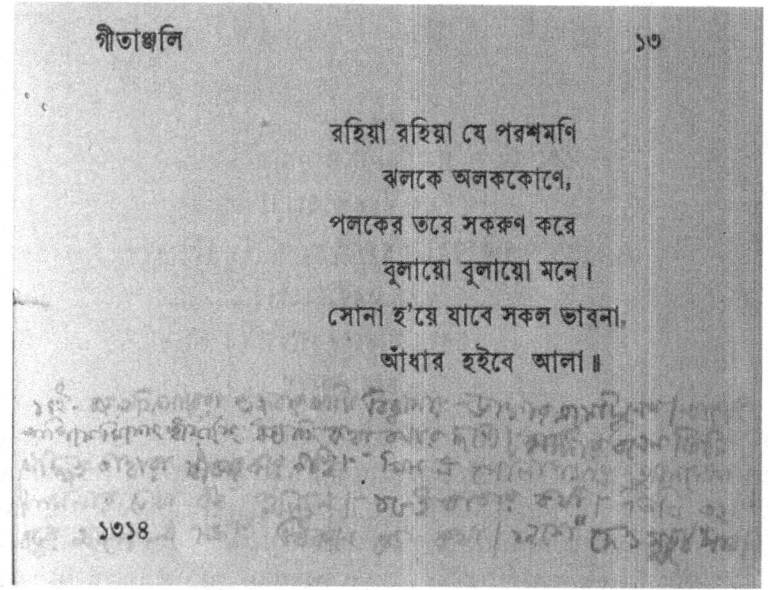

The final lines of Song 11

If one were to ask what Suhasini imbibed from Rabindranath, an answer may be found in Radhakrishnan's reflections on the poet's poetry and vision. As he notes, 'The artist helps us to forget the bonds with the world, and reveals to us the invisible connections by which we are bound up with eternity... The secret of all art lies in self-forgetfulness' (Radhakrishnan 1919, 122).

This 'self-forgetfulness' was not, for Suhasini, a form of escapism but a deliberate strategy—an effort to mobilise her inner resources, endure the harsh realities of camp life, and gather the strength to survive. In moments of pain, hunger and sorrow, she turned instinctively to poetry and song, which offered her glimpses of liberation, hope and harmony. These, in turn, reaffirmed her faith in the benevolent forces of the universe and enabled her to find beauty in small gestures of fraternity among strangers.

9

A British Indian Civilian

We know by now from the records that Suhasini had been listed as a British Indian civilian internee. But what did it mean for Suhasini to be categorised this way in the Fukushima internment camp roster? In pre-Independence days, this meant that she was a British subject, an Indian living in colonised, imperial India. As had been the case during the First World War, the outbreak of the Second World War once again meant global polarisation. The big three—Britain, the United States and the Soviet Union—constituted the Allied powers while the Axis powers that formed the opposing alliance were chiefly Japan, Germany and Italy. As a colonised nation, India's soldiers were compelled to fight under the British flag. This was also the period when the nationalist movement in India was gaining momentum, culminating in the 1942 call for the British to 'Quit India'—a demand that signified the end of British hegemony and renewed the bid for full self-governance, or *Purna Swaraj*, first articulated in the 1930 resolution.[1]

---

[1] At the December 1929 Lahore session of the Indian National Congress convention, a resolution was passed demanding complete self-governance (*Purna Swaraj*) rather than Dominion Status as envisaged earlier. This was formally announced on 26 January 1930, and was a significant event in the non-violent struggle for Indian independence.

Suhasini seems to have secretly kept herself informed about the political events unfolding in British India and the progressive milestones in the country's struggle for liberation. As prisoners in the camp, she and other inmates had no access to newspapers or information about the larger world. News trickled in only when one of the prisoners who could read Japanese was able to get hold of the previous day's newspaper, read the headlines in the lavatory and report to his fellow internees bits and pieces of news. For a short time after the Red Cross 'discovered' them, the internees had limited access to newspapers. But on 15 May 1945, Round notes, *Informed that there will be no more newspapers given to us*. Even when the Japanese surrender was imminent, on 16 July 1945 Round writes, *'The Japs do not give us news of the outside world. They try their best to keep us in the dark. But often we can tell by their mood whether the news is bad or not. We can read them like a book.'*

The opening lines of the Prologue in historian Ramachandra Guha's book *Rebels Against the Raj: Western Fighters for India's Freedom* observes, 'Loyalty is a virtue much cherished by humans, and those who are disloyal often face criticism. In the modern world, the gold standard of loyalty is loyalty to one's nation' (2022, xiii). He goes on to add, however, that occasionally history and morality encourage individuals to invest their allegiance elsewhere. In the case of Suhasini, who came from a Bengali Christian family, she was fully aware of the 'cultural-ideological struggle, represented by the socio-religious movements' that were 'an integral part of the evolving national consciousness' (Chandra 2000). The early intellectual and cultural interventions introduced by colonialism were met with national resistance on a different plane. The ideological conflict with hegemonic practices shaped both the politics of nationalism and its vision of a modern India. Suhasini found herself in a double dilemma. She could not, in any sense, support Japan's actions or policies; as an enemy power, its brutal treatment of civilian prisoners in the camp reflected poorly on both its conduct and its sense of humanity. At the same time, she remained indebted to her liberal education, which had nurtured the modern outlook that informed her efforts to improve the condition of women in India. Her loyalty to the British was therefore not a betrayal of the nationalist fervour that sustained the freedom movement in colonial India.

Her ambiguous and therefore difficult position is evident in Suhasini's exercise-book entry for 26 December 1943, which refers to an inquisition held in a small room next to the office. Annie Law, an elderly British missionary, and Suhasini were questioned for over two hours. The Camp Commandant was likely to have been present but it was the elderly interpreter, Midori Kawa who was directing his incisive and provocative questions to the two women. Suhasini writes in Bengali:

> Wanted to know everything. Asked me questions about each member of my family, incisive queries about myself. I told him only as much as was necessary. Wanted to know my elder brother's address—didn't give it. About home and work. Then started off about the British, that they had not done anything for India, they have kept people illiterate, Calcutta has been bombed.

> I became anxious, he told me, 'Why are our sons laying down lives, just for this. For rescuing Asia from their clutches. In India so many are dissatisfied, so many are anti-British, you must be knowing, there is frequent unrest among Hindus and Muslims. You are very ignorant, this is their strategy—they incite one community against another so that their purpose is fulfilled. You don't know anything, only busy with students.'

> I told them, 'I do not dabble in politics. I don't have anything to say against them. The school in which I was educated, it was very good education. Have a lot of British friends.

We will get self-government in time; we have got limited regional self-government.'

Then they started repeatedly saying that I knew nothing about the faults of the British. 'All your brothers and sisters work in good positions in British government organisations, what news will you have of the country.'

I was not willing to say anything much, I tried to pass it off with a yes or no. Hearing about bombing Calcutta, I told them that my elderly mother was there—just to turn the conversation.

Then Midori asked, 'Didn't you read newspapers at home?'

I said, 'Why wouldn't I read newspapers. I didn't get much time. I was busy with social upliftment and other work. The church etc.'

'These missionaries of yours are the main culprits—there are no greater liars than them. Missionary schools all do the work of spies, you don't know, we have proved that. You are not at all patriotic.'

So I replied, 'How do you know that I don't love my country—shall I give you an example? If I can buy three kinds of goods in the market, Indian, British and Japanese—do you know which I would buy? Indian made, if I need to, British made and then if I have no other choice then the Japanese. I don't spend even one paise of my hard-earned money without thinking where it is being spent.'

'We are trying to introduce new rules in the eastern provinces. If in this campaign we give you freedom, how are you going to help us?'

I replied, 'Keeping the campaign out of it, if you give us freedom, I will go back home and become engaged in teaching and social work, that kept me so busy earlier. Otherwise, there is not much else I can do for the country.'

'You are too pro-British.'

Eventually Midori said, 'Go back and change your mind otherwise all your facilities will be withdrawn. We are asking you how you are going to help us, why are you so biased towards the British?' Then I said, 'You are repeatedly asking me this. If the captain doesn't misunderstand me and excuse me, I know what it is to be under British rule. If I were to be under Japanese domination, I can say this much that the British know how to behave with women, the Japanese don't know that. In this way we are lucky.'

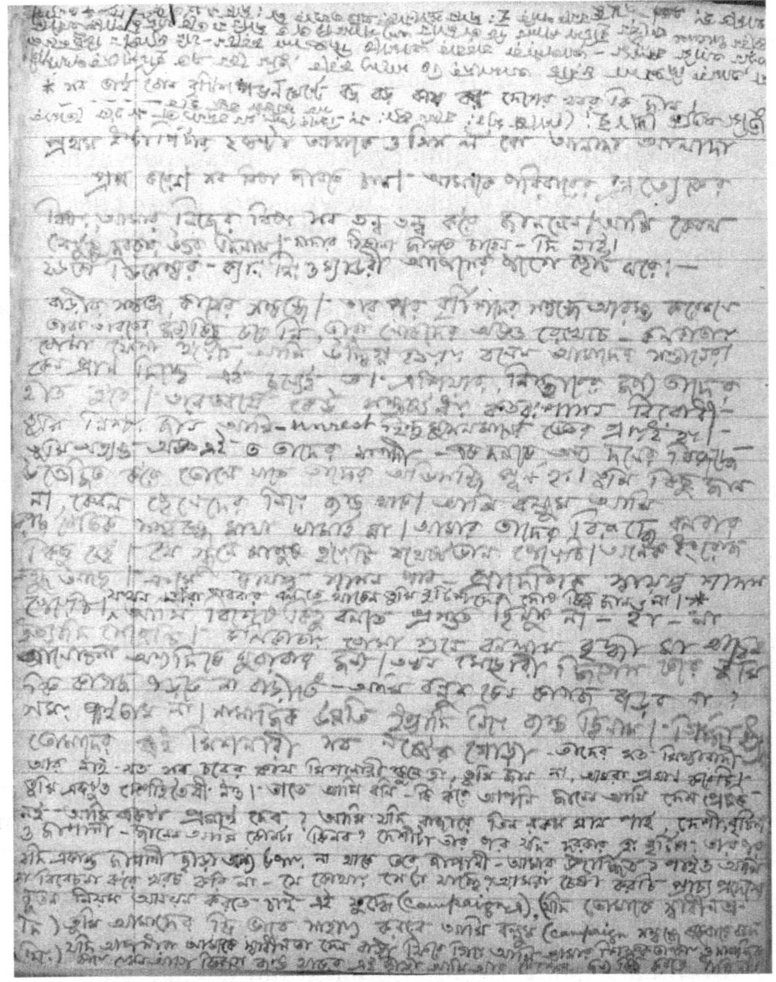

Suhasini's diary entry for 26 December 1943 mentioning the inquisition

The grit, determination and ideological clarity displayed by Suhasini is remarkable. Her interest in India's struggle for independence included an open letter composed by her, dated 3 May 1944, addressed to Subhas Chandra Bose. Those were the heady days of the Azad Hind Fauj under the charismatic leadership of Subhas Chandra Bose and Rashbehari Bose.[2] Their sphere of activity was Tokyo and Singapore, which afforded a strategic position from where they could amass troops to infiltrate into British India, in a bid to liberate the motherland. Suhasini expresses her thoughts in Bengali, writing a cramped hand on blue letter paper:

> Earlier I have had no particular reason to think about you. I have read whatever I had the opportunity to come across that was reported about the Congress in newspapers. If I had to board a tram for Pocha Bazar from Bhawanipur I have had to pass by your house; so, your house and that neighbourhood, my home and its neighbourhood can indeed be envisaged as a shared neighbourly ambience. We are both children of the same *Bangamata*. Therefore, as soon as I reached this country, I have been identified as a person belonging to Bose's own country. But whenever your name came up in the prisoner camp uttered by the captain, doctor or gardener, each time it pierced my heart like an arrow. Why did you choose to be honoured in a high position in this Japan and why are you not my co-prisoner in a prison camp? Why are you not going to be remembered by the Japanese along with the likes of me? It will be a matter of great regret the day one discovers what has driven you to this path—the greed for recognition by the Japanese or selfless love for the motherland. In this country your name has been spoken before me, but before this (March

---

[2] Rashbehari Bose (1886–1945) was an Indian revolutionary leader and freedom fighter. He avoided arrest by British intelligence by escaping to Japan in 1915, where he lived and died having been granted Japanese citizenship in 1923. He established the Indian Independence League in 1942 and invited Subhash Chandra Bose to join it as President.

1944) I did not realise how much damage you had done to our own country. The reason being that after abandoning your Bhawanipur home (disguised as a Buddhist monk), you have sometimes been in Berlin city, in Tokyo, and sometimes I have read in Australian newspapers about your accidental death in a plane crash. I have sometimes wondered, that for serving the motherland he has joined the enemy camp and in the end this is the outcome! But then I did not feel the disappointment that I feel now when I see Japanese newspapers flashing your name, your photographs your achievements, a fellow Bengali residing here. Then everyone asks these questions, who are you? Why are you thus incited? What is the West, what is the flag of Independent India and is the declaration of 'Azad Hind' the first step in declaring independence? Or is it the first step in his friend Japan's rising sun overrunning India? It is sad that a discerning man like you, defeated by the cleverness of those planning to grab your motherland, has been instrumental in the death of so many of your brothers. Their praise of you in their newspapers, your high standing, your army joining with the enemy country's and fighting on the motherland, seems unbearable. Today 3 May 1944, the World War completes five years. One hasn't heard much about you this last month. It may be that the defeat of the enemy in Burma has led to an ebb in the achievements and you have no work. I am letting you know some of my thoughts, now let me gauge what your thoughts are. If with the fall of Meiktila,[3] you have been taken prisoner by British soldiers, what happens to your call of *Dilli Chalo*[4] and raising the national flag there? Unfortunately, your brothers, your family must have had nightmarish times but one can tolerate everything for the

---

[3] The Battle of Meitkila was part of the Burma campaign from February to March 1945. The Allied forces won a decisive victory over the Japanese and the Indian National Army.

[4] This famous slogan was given by Subhas Chandra Bose in July 1943 at Padang, an open field in Singapore that has witnessed many historical events. He addressed several INA meetings there and also established a memorial for soldiers killed at the southern edge of the field.

good of one's country. But if today you are indeed a British prisoner, they will have to suffer anew what they had undergone before. I believe that I am almost at the end of my incarceration, but for you is it the beginning? When I was in the country, I did not have occasion to think about you, but now more and more I am worried about you. Let me not be remiss in accomplishing my duty towards the well-being of my country. At the end of my imprisonment may I love her even more. 23 January your birthday celebrations in Bangkok—43 years old...

Suhasini kept herself informed with the turns that the freedom movement was taking in India. In her exercise book, she had scribbled a note about the news of Netaji's death in an air crash in 1945, with no date, as well as 'Atom B' written in the lower left corner of the page. There are two small hand-sketched maps that indicate her interest in the progress of the war. It refers to the date 3 November 1944 when Netaji was to address a meeting in Tokyo. Cryptic words written on this page are '*Rani of Jhansi Regiment*', '*Capt. Lakshmi*', '*His Excellency S. Bose*', '*Flag, White, Saffron, Green*', '*Imphal*', '*1943 October, The Provisional Government*'. These randomly scribbled words can be pieced together as a phase in the Indian freedom movement featuring Subhas Chandra Bose who, in a broadcast over the Azad Hind Radio on 6 July 1944, addressed Mahatma Gandhi to say, 'India's last war of independence has begun . . . Father of our Nation! In this holy war of India's liberation, we ask for your blessing and good wishes' (Chandra 2000, 465).

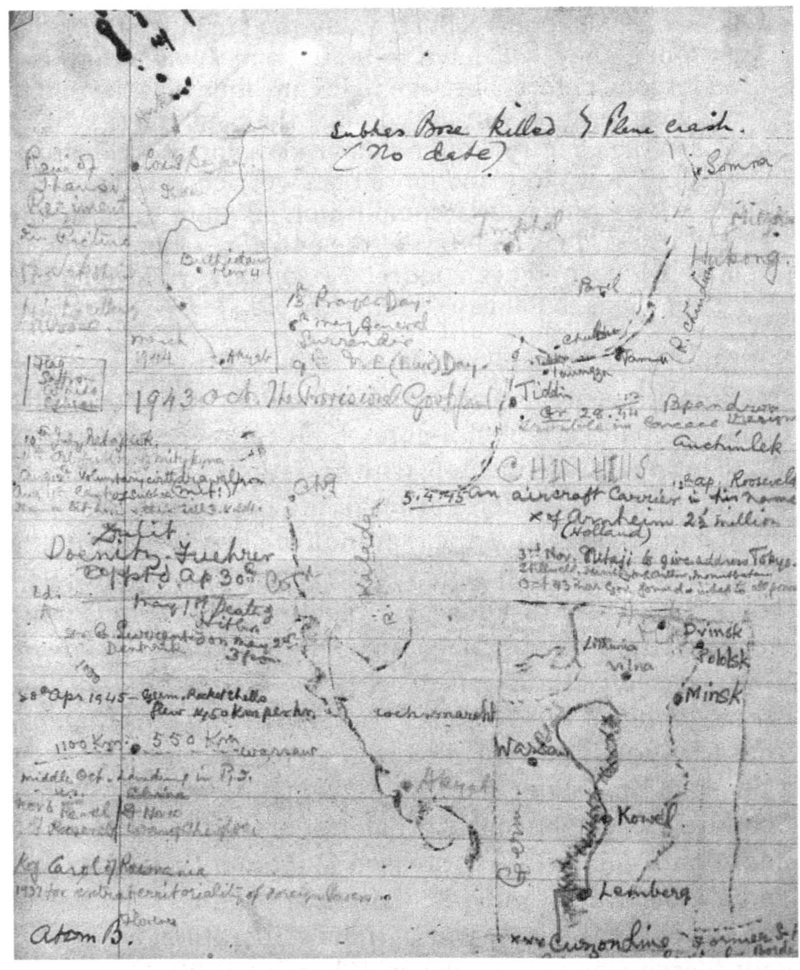

The notebook page containing Suhasini's scribblings about Netaji's death among other things

Several of Suhasini's 'markers' can be woven into the history of the second phase of the INA after Subhas Chandra Bose was brought to Singapore (2 July 1943) by German and Japanese submarines. Japanese Prime Minister Tojo reassured Bose at a meeting in Tokyo that Japan had no territorial designs on India. After Bose's return to Singapore, the Provisional Government of Free India was established on 21 October 1943 and was promptly recognised by the Axis powers. The reorganisation of the INA and the mobilisation of the Rani Jhansi regiment were taking place simultaneously. However, the discriminatory treatment meted out to the INA battalion commanded by Shah Nawaz Khan, which accompanied the Japanese army in the Imphal campaign, demoralised INA soldiers. The Imphal campaign failed, and the Japanese army began retreating in mid-1944, an ominous prelude to Japan's final surrender to the British in Southeast Asia.

Suhasini's notebook page also includes such 'markers' of the progress of the war in Europe. The death of Franklin D. Roosevelt, the 32nd President of the United States, on 12 April 1945 is noted. On 5 April 1945, there is an entry about an 'Am. aircraft carrier in his name'. The Battle of Arnheim, a major Allied intervention, took place from 17–25 September 1944. The plan to seize bridges across the Rhine was aborted by concerted German resistance. Suhasini records the casualty figure as an estimated '*2 and a half million*'.

After the First World War, the Curzon Line had demarcated the Second Polish Republic and the Soviet Union. When the Soviet Union invaded eastern Poland, this line became a major geopolitical issue during the Second World War. The division of Polish territory between the invading USSR and Nazi Germany along the Curzon Line was sealed by a secret pact. After the German attack on the Soviet Union in 1941, the Allies had to reach an agreement on Poland's future eastern border through post-war negotiations. The death of Hitler on 30 April 1945 is noted as a turning point in the war. Suhasini's entries, written close together, read: '*Doenitz Fuehrer apptd Ap 30th*' and immediately below that '*May 1st Death of Hitler*'.

Interestingly, this page brings together both the global sequence of advances and disasters that indicated the progression of the World War and the operations of the INA that were central to India's freedom struggle. What remained clear to Suhasini throughout her imprisonment was that her destiny and that of her camp-mates was inextricably linked to how and when the war ended.

10

Glimmerings of Hope

With the withdrawal of newspapers from the camp from May 1945 and the absence of regular radio access, the prisoners tried to piece together information from incidental sources—fragments of guards' conversations, rare occasions on which broadcasts could be overheard, and intuitive understanding of signs of airplane activity overhead.

From Round's entries it becomes obvious that the course of the war in 1944–45, Japan's consecutive defeats on the war front, and the food shortage on the domestic front, became matters of public interest in the Fukushima camp. His entry for 25 August 1944 records that '*Germany is in a bad way, so is Japan... Says Paris has fallen*'. In the early years of the war, Germany had overrun Luxembourg, the Netherlands and Belgium, and France had fallen soon after in June 1940. The Allied invasion of Normandy in June 1944 liberated France.

Despite the changing fortunes of the war, the bleak and cheerless camp life continued with its travails of insufficient and inedible food—buns gone sour or tea or soups that were nothing but hot water. Red Cross food parcels and clothes arrived on 25 and 26 September 1944—giving the internees something to rejoice about. The Japanese, however, remained brutally cruel, slapping punishments for flimsy reasons. For instance, on 23 October 1944 all the men were made to stand outside from 2–5 p.m. for refusing to run in the afternoon. In November and December 1944, there was a brief period of activity when the women were allowed to rehearse for a Christmas play. Everyone looked forward to a Christmas service, followed by concerts and plays and socialising among the men and women. Many nurtured the hope that the New Year would finally bring an end to the war. Yet, the Japanese wielded ruthless power over the internees. No effort was made to give medical attention to Mrs. Gleason, who died after a week of suffering. Punishments such as forcing an internee, Cecil Saunders, to stand with a bucket of water tied to his wrists, or the guards' random slapping of both men and women remained routine. Suhasini confessed her emotions of despair and longing in a short four-line Bengali poem found in her notebook:

When will this ordeal end
To my country I'll finally wend
Brothers, sisters, loved ones
Are watching the path ...

The poem Suhasini composed

Round's entry for 11 January 1945 records the American victory at Luzon when the Philippine Islands were wrested back from the Japanese. It was one of the bloodiest battles of the Pacific War and signalled the onset of Japan's fall. The battle stretched over two months, and Japan lost an estimated 55,000 troops or more since the operations began. On 31 January, the Russian forces had advanced to within fifteen miles of Berlin. The Allies' successive victories fostered a renewed sense of hope among the camp's prisoners. Their days from February 1945 onwards were punctuated by frequent air-raid sirens and alarms going off at all hours, which meant taking shelter in the boiler room, proceeding to the assembly room, accompanied by the constant sound of planes passing overhead. News trickled in not only of the Americans entering Manila but also of raids on Tokyo, and on Kanto in the Honshu region closer to Fukushima.

An air raid in the morning of 22 April 1945 helped the inmates identify an American aircraft passing at considerable altitude and remarkable speed overhead. The fear of annihilation by atomic bombs was not entirely absent from their thoughts, while the frequent earthquakes and tremors—sometimes quite severe—further underscored the fragility of human life.

By the end of May 1945, it was clear to the prisoners that Japan's invasion was imminent. With communication networks with the outside world blocked, the prisoners learnt to read the behaviour of the Japanese staff in the camp, and also study the airspace activity of identified or unidentified military aircraft to conclude that '*outstanding signs point to it [invasion of Japan]*' (Round's entry on 30 May 1945). By July, the prisoners had become restless, looking forward to the Americans landing soon. It would mean liberation and perhaps the end of the war.

This atmosphere of relief, however, was not without a sense of apprehension, as an entry in Round's diary for 20 July 1945 indicates. Sleep had been impossible the previous night and, in the morning, there was more air activity:

> A plane dived out of the clouds and dropped a single bomb less than a mile from our building, away over to the South East. Before the bomb was released the plane scouted around for a while. All of us were looking out of the windows trying to catch a glimpse of it. We could tell by its engines that it was not a Jap.

Such bombing raids could easily catch the prisoners unawares, placing both the incarcerators and the incarcerated at risk of perishing. The Japanese themselves were visibly afraid—scattering when the bomb exploded, diving swiftly into their shelters to save themselves, with even the Camp Commandant shaking in fear. The valley was shrouded with low-lying clouds, a picture of misery and despair. Most internees, despite their unwavering faith in God, wondered whether they would survive to tell their stories to the people at home.

The internees expected that the invasion of Japan would be accomplished within the following month. This would serve to be almost prophetic, one could say. Everyone's health had deteriorated as food supplies were meagre—actually significantly insufficient—consisting of dirty, tasteless three-and-a-half buns for breakfast, lunch, and tea, washed down with hot water, for the so-called tea or soup served was nothing more than that. Yet the internees no longer minded the deprivation, as they hoped the Americans would soon restore them to proper health. For Suhasini and most of the others who had held fast to faith, this prevailing darkness, despair, and perplexity was a trial of faith; they believed that Christ, the Prince of Light, stood beside them, offering succour amid a deeply joyless environment. Smaller mercies of receiving letters, cables, and news from home, seemed insignificant beside this persistent vision of imminent liberation.

This vision that was close to becoming a much-desired reality is articulated in this poem composed in the camp by the irrepressible 'Miss S. Curtis'[1]

Freedom
Oh to be free once more
Free like the lark to soar,
Up towards the sky,
Singing his joyful song
Happy the whole day long.

<u>Happy and free</u>.
Once more to roam the hills,
Wanderings where fancy wills
Just to be <u>free</u>.
Following the errant stream,
Watching the sunshine gleam,
Happy and <u>free</u>!
Oh to be free again,
Free like the wind and rain.
Playthings of Heaven.
Solitude and peace be mine
God given gifts divine,
Let me be free.

---

[1] The poems (Ms. 99/31/1, Imperial War Museum, London) were written on a letter-pad, on one side of the page.

11

End of War and Freedom

Freedom and the end of the global war came at a heavy cost. On 6 August 1945, the United States, acting on President Harry Truman's orders, unleashed the world's first atomic bomb on Hiroshima. The prisoners at Fukushima had scrambled to their shelters at 8 a.m. that day; the sirens blared again at 9.15, followed by an all-clear a little after noon. Though they heard the airplanes overhead, they had no way of knowing if anything had been dropped. It was, however, a massive, incomprehensible devastation of human lives.

After two fairly uneventful nights, 9 August 1945 dawned in the camp with early morning sirens that sent the camp into its usual scramble for shelter. Planes could be heard a little later at 7.45 a.m., and to the far northeast there seemed to be distant bombings. Anti-aircraft guns sounded briefly, and planes passed high over the valley. Throughout the day, explosions could be heard in the distance towards the south, while planes roared overhead. The internees remained in the shelter for six hours and five minutes from mid-morning, and even the Japanese peasants working in the surrounding fields fled instantly at the warning. At times, the prisoners were not sure whether the distant rumbling was thunder or exploding bombs. Unbeknownst to them, the commercial city and seaport of Nagasaki had been bombed, killing 40,000 people instantly, with another 40,000 dying soon after from injuries, burns, and radiation exposure. Many more would bear the physical and emotional scars of this inhumane act for decades.

Alfred Round's entries for the next three days show that camp life had become tense as both the Japanese and the internees seemed to be waiting for something; an eerie stillness shrouded the atmosphere. Although the prisoners longed for peace, it was difficult to discern what the inscrutable Japanese staff in the camp were thinking. Historical events reveal that after the two consecutive atomic bombings, Japan was in deep turmoil. Even after the Nagasaki bombing—despite America keeping atomic bombs in reserve for further action—Japan's war council and cabinet that met on the afternoon of 9 August, continued to debate the question of surrender. Although hopes of victory had largely receded, several members were of the opinion that the war should continue. Since no unanimous decision could be reached, the issue was referred to the imperial palace. The Emperor supported convening an imperial conference, and though consensus was difficult, he indicated that the Foreign Minster Shigenori Tōgō should let the Allies know that Japan would accept the terms of surrender on the condition that the *kokutai*[1] be preserved. Emperor Hirohito recorded his address to the nation on 14 August 1945, announcing Japan's decision to capitulate to the Allies. Though the military establishment was not in favour of this surrender, the recorded speech was finally broadcast on 15 August 1945.

At the camp on 15 August 1945, the mandatory morning roll call was underway when the air-raid sirens suddenly sounded. The guards told the gathered prisoners that the

---

[1] *Kokutai* in Japanese translates to sovereignty, national polity or identity.

Americans were deploying a new kind of bomb, dropped by parachutes, which caused vast destruction on exploding. The uncertainty was deeply unsettling for the prisoners. That morning, they also witnessed a strange incident: the Japanese staff had gathered in the office, listening intently to a radio broadcast. When the speech ended, the Japanese national anthem was played, and Obasan—the elderly wife of the camp cook—was in tears. It became obvious to the camp survivors that the Emperor himself had spoken on the radio, and they hoped desperately it had something to do with peace.

The Japanese officials, guards and staff remained tight-lipped, withholding any information. It was only the next morning, when a Japanese paper was quietly sneaked upstairs into the rooms, that the internees finally heard the splendid news that the war with Japan had indeed come to an end. Round's entry recorded the moment: *'The whole camp was in an uproar—people shaking hands, kissing each other for joy'*. Finally at 11.30 a.m., they were all summoned to the Greek room into which they walked freely. Although the guards attempted to conduct a roll call, the internees refused to comply. The announcement of Japan's surrender was curtly made.

By evening, the sergeant's demeanour had noticeably softened. He expressed sympathy for what the internees had endured and blamed circumstances for the cruelty meted out to them. His sudden shift in behaviour may have been at attempt at back-tracking, for although Japan had accepted the laws codified by the Geneva Convention on the Prisoners of War in 1929, the ground realities of life in the camp had been far from its standards. Round writes, *'It is a fact that it is an absolute miracle the way we have been preserved throughout the 3 bitter years of bondage.'*

After news of the surrender, several days passed before the formal documents were signed aboard the *USS Missouri* on 2 September 1945, a date officially designated as the official Victory over Japan Day (V–J Day). With this, the World War came to an end both in Europe and Asia. Hardly any part of the world had escaped the devastation, brutality, carnage, genocide, horror, and tragedy it unleashed. The Holocaust and the atrocities of Auschwitz remain among the gravest crimes against humanity. The atomic bombs, "Little Boy" and "Fat Man" that decimated civilian populations and left a trail of debilitating radiation on generations to come, exposed the ugly face of political power.

Though various countries constituted war-crimes tribunals, the jurisdiction and scope of international humanitarian laws remained ambiguous. The effectiveness of the Nuremberg Trials or the Tokyo Trials are much debated. Notably, Justice Radha Binod Pal (1886–1957),[2] representing the British Commonwealth on the International Military Tribunal of the Far East (IMTFE), issued a strong dissent when the Tokyo Trials delivered their verdict after more than two and a half years of deliberations. He argued that the USA's nuclear bombings of Hiroshima and Nagasaki should themselves be classified a heinous crime against humanity.

The treatment of civilian prisoners of war at Fukushima—including children—through starvation, humiliation, and harsh punishment clearly constituted as criminal atrocities under the provisions of the Geneva Convention. Even otherwise, withholding medical aid or not providing basic hygienic conditions, and withdrawing all forms of freedom in terms of speech or movement amounted to severe violations of human rights. As Freud observed, the trauma endured by such survivors extended far beyond physical wounds, and would cause deep psychological scars. This

---

[2] https://www.nationalww2museum.org/war/articles/justice-radhabinod-pal-tokyo-war-crimes-trial. Accessed on 10 January 2026.

'breach in the mind's experience of time, self, and the world—is not, like the wound of the body, a simple and healable event', writes Cathy Caruth (1996, 5).

Yet each survivor tried to cope in his/her own way. It was not the disruptions that they noticed now, but the continuities. Liberation felt like a brief poetic interlude—when one connected to the life of nature, trying to find soothing peace after months of experiencing and witnessing human hatred and violence. Their experience almost echoed Thomas Hardy's words,[3] *'Yonder a maid and her wight/ Come whispering by/ War's annals will cloud into night/ Ere their story die'*. Round exults: *'The peasants continued to labour in the rice fields, the frogs their noisy croaking, and the beautiful mountains were the same as ever, towering in majestic beauty and splendour above the green fertile valley looking down on the white convent...'*

Freedom had brought with it a deepening of faith, a profound sense of gratitude, and joyous enjoyment of life itself. On 22 August 1945, the entire camp gathered in front of the building—bearing memories of three and a half years—to be captured in two separate group photographs.

---

[3] Thomas Hardy (1840–1928), In Time of 'Breaking of Nations' https://www.poetryfoundation.org/poems/57320/in-time-of-the-breaking-of-nations. Accessed on 8 January 2026.

Images courtesy Michael Charnaud

The group photographs taken at the Fukushima camp. Suhasini can be seen in a sari, in the left corner of the first picture

Image courtesy Roger Mansell

Aerial view of the POW camp at Fukushima

The internees were now eagerly awaiting their return home. They were thrilled at the sight of American or British planes flying overhead, and on the morning of 25 August, when twelve single-engined American planes swooped and roared over the camp, the prisoners rushed out cheering and waving. Later that afternoon, the Americans dropped food supplies, waving from their cockpits and dipping their wings in acknowledgment of the cheering from the ground. Relief supplies continued to be air-dropped in the days that followed, and there was great enthusiasm among the internees.

On 28 August, however, tragedy struck unexpectedly during one such supply drop. The Greek radio officer Dimitolskopulos' wife was injured and taken to hospital, where she later died. The unfortunate incident sent shock waves through the camp. Even at the moment of relief, the internees were reminded of mortality and transience of human life. Suhasini had her own way of negotiating mortality, and in her one-on-one interaction with Tagore's Song 117 (Bengali)[4], she wrote at the top of the page, '*At one time I was not afraid of death. But I don't know why, suddenly I saw it in a different way.*' The song reads as follows:

> I am a traveller, friend,
> None can keep me tied.
> False are the bonds of joy and sorrow,
>   this home will be left behind...
> Material burdens drag me down, they will be cast away...
> I will move beyond good or evil, from this to other worlds.
> I am a traveller, friend,
> All burdens left behind,
> The sky calls me from afar in unknown wordless songs. (Tagore 2023, 103)

---

[4] *Jatri ami ore/parbe na keu rakhte amay dhore*

12

The Long Journey Home

On 11 September 1945, with barely an hour and a half's notice, the prisoners were instructed to prepare to leave for the railway station; they were subsequently put on a train heading north towards Sendai. As it trundled through rural Japan, the internees caught glimpses of valleys nestled between forested hills, stretches of ripening paddy fields, and green orchards, until they arrived at the fishing town of Shiogama. The buildings were in ruins, a result of American offshore shelling, and they picked their way through the rubble, guided by American volunteers, to the seashore. The first night away from camp was spent aboard a USS Hospital Ship anchored mid-harbour. The next morning, after a heavy early breakfast, they boarded the Australian destroyer HMAS *Warrumunga*, bound for Yokohama. The ship travelled at full speed and reached the designated port by 4 p.m. The newly liberated prisoners were then transferred for the night to a large Landing Ship Tank (LST) fitted with bunks and camp beds. They were well cared for, receiving both dinner and breakfast before being transferred once again, this time to a modest British ship, the *Ruler*, which was carrying almost 445 rescued POWs in addition to an existing complement of 600, and was scheduled to sail for Sydney. The ship finally set sail on 14 September and entered Sydney Harbour on 27

September 1945 to a rousing welcome, as it was the first vessel bringing POWs home.

For Suhasini, the journey back to India still lay far ahead. In her letter dated 18 September 1945, her elder sister Surama expresses her relief and thankfulness to God for answering their prayers, wonders whether any money should be sent, and mentions that she was going on a tour (as Inspectress of Schools) but hoped to be back in time to welcome Suhasini home. Excitement about Suhasini's liberation and homecoming was equally high both in India and Australia.

In a letter dated 29 September 1945, H. G. Redman of Adelaide writes, '*Your safe return is an answer to many prayers from your friends scattered all over Australia and India. Our daughter Jess I understand received a note or message from you.*'

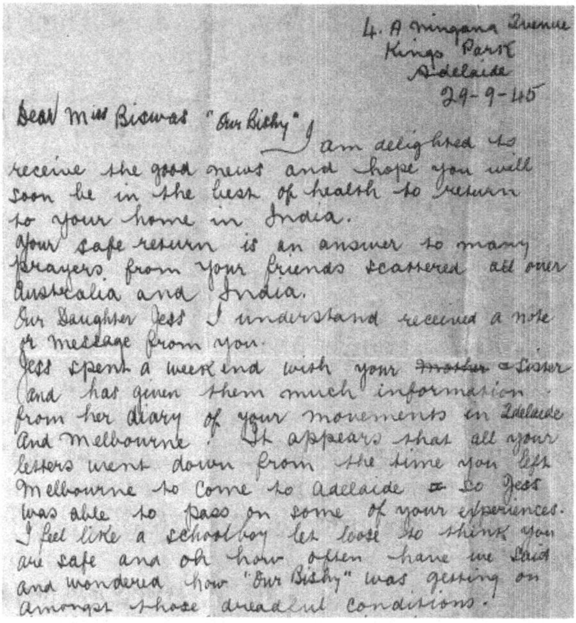

Redman's letter to Suhasini

According to his advice, the best way to cope with memories of *'those dreadful conditions'* would be an *'endeavour to forget the past and wish the joy of coming through safe, commence to again be happy and enjoy the so long lost pleasures of living'*. The letter also included an open invitation to Suhasini to stay with them while she waited to be booked on a passage home, for it must have been a real disappointment not to have been taken straight home after her release. It went on to express the hope: *'If you get a boat almost straight away to your beloved homeland, I wish you a very happy voyage and feel that the sea journey will work wonders in restoring you to a normal health in readiness for a rousing welcome home'*.

Sometime in November 1945, Suhasini's elder brother, S. K. Biswas—recently retired and living in New Delhi—wrote to his dear sister that the best news they had heard in many years was that of her release, and they were relieved their prayers had been answered. Their joy knew no bounds, and he spoke of how *'a hearty welcome awaits you'*. The inland letter was addressed to the Australian Army Base Post Office in Melbourne and was redirected to Miss Cousin in Ashfield, New South Wales. In an age of slow communications, the letter reached much after Suhasini had left Australia and there was a time gap in gauging her travel movements.

A letter dated 7 October 1945, written by Helen O. Cousin, mentions seeing Suhasini off on her homeward journey aboard the *Otranto*, which left the Sydney Harbour on the same day, calling at Fremantle before proceeding to Bombay. After leaving the wharf, Helen made the effort to go to the post office and send a cable to Suhasini's family in Calcutta. In another letter dated 16 October 1945, she expresses surprise at *'How quickly you got to Fremantle'* and reiterates the hope of a swift return: *'It looks as if it won't be many more days before you are in India; you should be right home well before the end of the month. What a time of rejoicing that will be! The arrival of the "Ruler" will be nothing to that arrival'.*

62 Service Avenue,
Ashfield, N.S.W.
Australia,
16·10·'45.

My dear Suhasini,

How quickly you got to Fremantle! We could scarcely believe it when Mrs Hale rang to say she had received your cable — no wire. And then your air letter came! It looks as if it won't be many more days before you are in India; you should be right home well before the end of the month. What a time of rejoicing that will be! The arrival of the "Ruler" will be nothing to that arrival.

Cousin's letter to Suhasini, dated 16 October 1945

Paradoxically, Suhasini reached Bombay earlier than expected. Two undated picture postcards featuring the General Post Office and the offices of the Government of India—never meant to be posted—are inscribed in pencil in Bengali, expressing her emotions on returning to her own country after almost four years. There is a deep sense of disappointment when she writes:

> I had heard about the city of Bombay, and now I am seeing it firsthand. Yet, I am unable to enjoy anything here because though it may not be [as foreign] as a Japanese port, it is almost like coming to land at the Australian harbour as I cannot see any of my family here, nor is the environment here at all familiar.

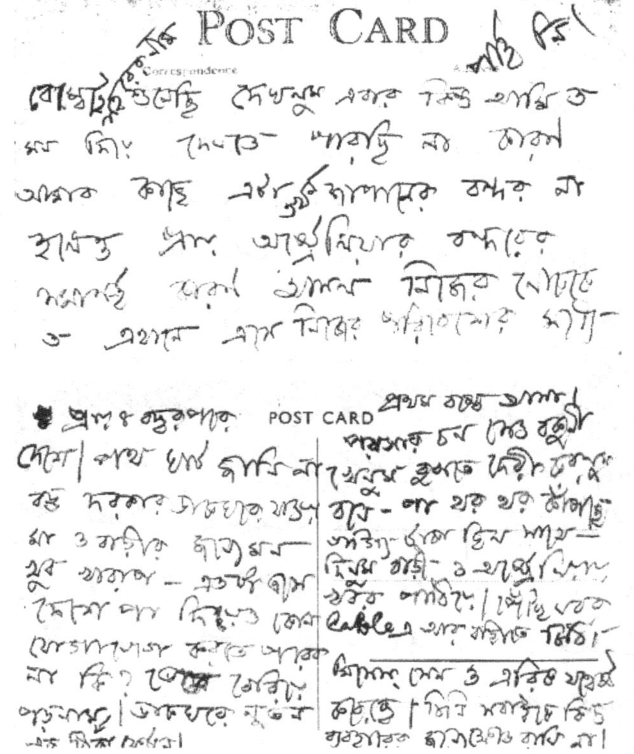

The two postcards written by Suhasini but never posted

In another entry, Suhasini rues the fact that

> I am back to my country after almost 4 years. It is my first Bombay visit. I don't know the roads and lanes, yet I need to go to the post office urgently. I am feeling too homesick especially for my mother and the family. Though I am back in my own country after a long long journey, will I not be able to communicate with them at all? These were my thoughts as I set out in a hired 'phaeton gari' in search of the post office. In the post office new currency is being used—they were impatient that it took me some time to figure out the new coins—my legs are trembling— luckily I had some money with me—sent news home and to Australia. News of safe arrival by cable, and a letter home.

In these days of effortless global communication, it is difficult to fully comprehend the trauma, ordeals, and anxieties that Suhasini endured. She was in her own country, yet still miles away from her loved ones; Bombay must have felt like another universe. She does, however, mention Indian friends who cared for her until her brother, delayed by miscommunication or late news, was finally able to travel and accompany her by train to Calcutta.

The city of her birth must have appeared very different on her arrival from when she had left. It bore the scars of war, bombings and air raids, and though not always visible on the surface of the metropolis, it had suffered the worst man-made famine that had claimed millions of lives. Nationalist forces were in conflict with the colonial masters, and there was an overall atmosphere of restlessness. The change of government in the United Kingdom, with the Labour Party coming to power and Clement Attlee becoming Prime Minister, signalled steps towards granting self-rule to colonised India. The country was far from peaceful; Suhasini hoped to return to Comilla and resume her job after the New Year, but the shadows of the impending Partition loomed large.

However, Suhasini's arrival was a time of deep family rejoicing, of returning to her mother who had patiently prayed for her homecoming. There were new faces—nephews and nieces—eager to welcome her back. Letters of thanksgiving poured in from friends in Australia, Dacca, Comilla, Brahmanberia, and other Baptist centres. Christmas was celebrated joyfully, at last, with family after her long and arduous exile.

Epilogue

After her return to India, and having spent Christmas with her family in Calcutta, it was time for Surama to return to Dhaka and her work. Suhasini chose to go back with her sister, looking forward to rejoining her old school in Comilla. She needed time to recover physically after her harrowing years of internment in adverse health conditions. Nutritious and adequate portions of food had not been part of the daily rations, and as we have seen, several of her marginal entries speak of hunger pangs. A comparative table of weights compiled by researchers[1] shows that Suhasini had lost 25 pounds by the end of her internment. Since her hair had also fallen out, those who remembered her from that time called her 'Nedu Mashi'. Medical treatment had been persistently denied by the Japanese commandants. Suhasini's repeated complaints of toothache were neglected or hastily dismissed; as a result, she had lost several teeth and had visibly aged during her years in captivity.

Once in Dhaka, she spent long spells of time in the Rankin Street (old Dhaka) home of their family friend Shantiprapha Nag, elder sister of Suprabha Dasgupta, headmistress of Khastagir Girls' School, Chittagong. This was largely because Surama Biswas often had to travel out of town

---

[1] https://www.pegasusarchive.org/pow/cJpFukushima.htm The table in Appendix IV shows the inmates' weights in pounds before capture, three months after internment in Japan, and at the end of their internment. It has been compiled from signed statements by the internees themselves.

for school inspections. Suhasini spent much of 1946–47 in this supportive family environment, slowly recovering her broken-down health.

In the sequence of events leading up to the political independence of the country, the partition of India became imminent. Several families, including the Nag household, were compelled to relocate to Calcutta. Surama too moved to newly independent India to join the Refugee Rehabilitation Department in Calcutta. Suhasini joined Sakhawat Memorial Girls' School (established in 1911 by Rokeya Sakhawat Hossain) as its headmistress. She retired in 1950 and thereafter devoted herself selflessly to social work for the uplift of homeless women and children with the All Bengal Women's Union (established in 1933).

Image courtesy Ratnabali Ray

Suhasini at her retirement in 1950

Suhasini was characterised by her indomitable courage, deep devotion to her faith, and a quiet resilience that saw her through the Fukushima ordeal. She maintained a low profile during the trying camp days, helping internees resolve misunderstandings, quietly expressing solidarity with the women who had been slapped, punched, punished or manhandled by the Japanese guards who constantly intruded on their privacy. Her responsibilities included contributing time and expertise to teaching the children in the camp. Her notebook carries pages of tasks like math exercises and moral lessons meant for the young. Camp inmates trusted her with the safekeeping of the sparse provisions allotted to them before and after the Red Cross International visits, a trust clearly reflected in the meticulous inventories she created in her notebook.

The fact that Suhasini did not write any account about her traumatic experiences indicates that she was reluctant to revisit this phase of her life. Coming to terms with her present seemed more meaningful, and her compassionate social work helped heal a small part of her lingering mental wounds. As an archive, the *Gitanjali* in which she chronicled significant everyday events inside the Fukushima camp serves as a micro-history of how the Second World War impacted civilian life, migration, and futures globally. Almost everyone emerged from the camp psychologically scarred. Suhasini was deeply affected, but instead of adopting a confessional mode in her marginalia, she used her voice to reflect on ethics and compassion, cruelty and punishment, religious belief, and simple humaneness in wartime.

A few days after I had written a draft (in 2015) for what now appears as the Prologue to this book, I came upon 'The Charnaud Family Website' set up by Michael Charnaud, who was the ten-year-old boy travelling with his mother, Madeline Charnaud, on the ill-fated *SS Nankin* in 1942 from Australia to Ceylon. Delighted and thrilled to have discovered this website, I reached out to Michael by email. He responded promptly: '*Glad to make your acquaintance. I well remember Miss Biswas and I will help you in any way possible*' (20 August 2015). I had already read his first-person account of life in the camp in the BBC War Archives,[2] and now I was in direct contact with a former internee! In his next mail, he attached two group photographs taken in the camp in August 1945, after the war had ended. The young Michael was clearly visible, identified for my convenience. Miss Biswas also appears in the photograph, and Michael added, '*Miss Biswas—I remember her as teaching a lot of the smaller ones basic reading, arithmetic etc.*'

In the same email he sent lovely photographs of himself and his wife Jill—his companion of over sixty years—as well as of their dog, in their country home in Surrey. He looked jovial and well in the photographs, and when I remarked on this, he wrote, '*There is no one else as far as I am aware still surviving from those days... I am only still going because I walk my 3 dogs 2 miles first thing every morning whether it is sunny, raining, snowing etc. and I have a large 4-acre garden!*'

Image courtesy Michael Charnaud

Michael Charnaud at 93 with his dog Percy at his Surrey home

---

2 https://www.bbc.co.uk/history/ww2peopleswar/stories/79/a4220579.shtml

This email correspondence gave new impetus to telling the story of 'Miss Biswas'. I called Michael and had a pleasant conversation with him—his memory remarkably sharp and his voice wonderfully vibrant. I had spoken first-hand to a survivor of the camp, someone who remembered Suhasini Biswas! I asked him a few questions: Were there any other British Indians in the camp? Was Miss Biswas always in a saree? After the war ended, did they travel together on the same ship to Bombay en route to Colombo? Michael's answers were clear and simple. Details of life in the camp were firmly etched in his mind. There were no other British Indians besides Miss Biswas. She was indeed always in a saree. They did not travel on the same ship to Bombay, as his mother Madeline had secured an earlier passage back to Colombo via Bombay from Sydney Harbour.

I cannot but marvel at modern, technology-enabled communication that allowed me to write and speak to Michael, probably the last surviving member of the Fukushima Civilian Internment Camp. In April 2007, Michael's son Paul, his grandsons Joe and Louis, friends Cathy and James, along with Sarah, visited Fukushima and the Convent, the site of the camp. They knew the hair-raising stories Michael had narrated, yet they were struck by the major incongruity during the visit: the family carried an awareness of the misery, abuse and death that had occurred there, while the Convent sisters, who had lived in the place for over half a century, regarded it simply as their home and haven, oblivious of its painful and harrowing past.

Nearly a decade has passed between my conversation with Michael Charnaud and a subsequent exchange of emails, and now, as I attempt to bring this research to a close, I am confronted by certain stark realities. Sadly, my husband Sujoy, who was most deeply involved in my project, is no more. Several key figures, such as Roger Mansell and

Rod Suddaby, have also passed away. While updating the Epilogue, I also learnt from his son Paul, that Michael, having lived a full and active life had passed away in 2024. I have almost lost touch with Robert Murphy and some of the other Fukushima researchers. Their contributions to the POW network, luckily, still remain accessible on the worldwide web. After the 2011 earthquake, tsunami, and ensuing nuclear plant disaster in Fukushima, the Convent structure was declared unsafe and subsequently demolished.[3] In his dissertation, Robert Murphy notes his surprise at discovering that the very existence of the Fukushima POW camp during the war was unknown even to residents of the city.

Since 2011, it seems more than ever that these memoirs—linked to a massive worldwide upheaval—risk being lost forever. Only narratives documented by the BBC remain, along with a few accounts preserved by families in personal or institutional archives. Suhasini's personal story has been particularly vulnerable, as it was never formally documented. Her notes were largely written in Bengali, and she likely chose to distance herself from a trauma that had indelibly scarred her psyche. What she narrated to nephews, nieces or family and friends was never recorded as an oral archive. Retrieving an eyewitness account from near oblivion in an attempt to reconstruct the life and

---

[3] The Convent of Notre Dame in Fukushima is one of several buildings in the area that has been impacted by the 2011 nuclear disaster.

From a letter I received from Robert Murphy on 11 January 2024: *Fortunately, no friends or relatives in Japan were hurt in the two disasters, but they awakened deeply-felt memories seared into our very bones and nervous systems. We were trapped for a week in Fukushima after the massive 6-minute earthquake and tsunami on 11 March 2011, with resulting nuclear fallout. Incidentally, this earthquake seriously damaged the convent that had been used to house the POWs from 1942-1945, and it was demolished many months later.*

memories of a daring woman from the subcontinent has helped challenge formulaic notions about gender. This book—drawing on the forgotten experiences of a prisoner of war, including her remarkable conversations with the poems of one of India's foremost poet-philosophers—hopes to articulate the repressed anguish and infinite patience embedded in her scattered jottings. It is difficult to imagine how Suhasini would have reacted herself to the place, to the recalling, and to the telling if she had memorialised her own story either as a confessional or a testimonio.

The long years spent in deciphering the archival material, filling in gaps, and understanding the intersections of political alignments, national identities, and transnational encounters have been a profound learning experience. Over the course of this research, Suhasini emerged as a figure of hope and compassion, grounded in faith in divinity and belief in humanitarianism. Her story, caught in the throes of political and personal conflicts, ultimately celebrates the human spirit and offers some semblance of cathartic closure.

References

Caruth, Cathy. 1996. *Unclaimed Experience: Trauma, Narrative, and History*. Baltimore: Johns Hopkins University Press.

Chandra, Bipan. 2000. *India's Struggle for Independence, 1857–1947*. New Delhi: Penguin India.

Charnaud, M. 2005. "A Child's War, Parts 1–20." *BBC WW2 People's War*. http://www.bbc.co.uk/dna/ww2/A4220579.

Foucault, Michel. 1995. *Discipline and Punish: The Birth of the Prison*. Translated by Alan Sheridan. New York: Random House. Originally published 1977.

Guha, Ramachandra. 2022. *Rebels Against the Raj: Western Fighters for India's Freedom*. New Delhi: Penguin Random House.

Gupta, Jayati. n.d. "Fukushima Civilian Internment Camp." http://www.mansell.com/pow_resources/camplists/sendai/fukushima/fukushima.htm. Accessed November 17, 2025.

———. 2012. "Whose *Gitanjali* Is It Anyway?" *Muse India*, no. 45 (September–October).

The Holy Bible. 1984. New International Version. Colorado Springs: International Bible Society.

Reyes, Kathryn Blackmer, and Julia E. Curry Rodríguez. 2012. "Testimonio: Origins, Terms, and Resources." *Equity & Excellence in Education* 45, no. 3: 525–538. https://doi.org/10.1080/10665684.2012.698571.

Mansell, Roger. n.d. "Fukushima Civilian Internment Camp." http://www.mansell.com/pow_resources/camplists/sendai/fukushima/fukushima.htm. Accessed November

17, 2025.

Millar, Andy. 2012. *Lost at Sea: Found at Fukushima*. Big Sky Publishing.

Murphy, Robert G. 2006. "The Fukushima Civil Internment Camp, 1942–1945." MA dissertation, University of Sheffield.

Radhakrishnan, Sarvepalli. 1919. *The Philosophy of Rabindranath Tagore*. London: Macmillan and Company.

Saunders, Cecil. 2003. "Fukushima Civilian Internment Camp." *BBC WW2 People's War*. https://www.bbc.co.uk/history/ww2peopleswar/stories/13/a2021013.shtml. Accessed January 07, 2026.

Scott, M. I. 1945. "Fukushima Civilian Internment Camp, Japan, June 1945." http://www.cofepow.org.uk/pages/asia_japan_fukushima.htm. Accessed January 07, 2026.

Tagore, Rabindranath. 1925. *Gitanjali* (Bengali). Reprint. Santiniketan: Visva-Bharati.

———. 1977. *Gitanjali (Song Offerings)*. Reprint. New Delhi: Macmillan Company of India.

———. 2003. *Gitanjali (Song Offerings)*. New Delhi: UBS Publishers.

———. 2011. *Gitanjali (Song Offerings): A New Translation*. Translated by William Radice. New Delhi: Penguin.

———. 2012. *Gitanjali (Song Offerings): Bilingual Edition*. Collated and edited by Tapati Mukhopadhyay and Amrit Sen. Santiniketan: Rabindra-Bhavana, Visva-Bharati.

———. 2023. *Selected Rabindrasangeet in English Translation, vol. 1*. Translated by Indrani Haldar. Blue Pencil Publishing.

Thapar, Romila. 2000. *Narratives and the Making of History: Two Lectures*. New Delhi: Oxford University Press.

Jayati Gupta is an academic based in Kolkata. Her career spans over 44 years in undergraduate and postgraduate teaching and research in English Literary Studies. She has nurtured generations of students in the erstwhile Presidency College, Lady Brabourne College, the West Bengal State University, as guest faculty at the University of Calcutta and Visiting Professor at Adamas University. She was awarded the Tagore National Fellowship for Cultural Research by the Ministry of Culture, Government of India (2015–2017) and was attached to the National Library of India, Kolkata, during the tenure of the Fellowship. Her project titled 'The Cultures of Travel in Bengal' led to a book published by Routledge, U.K. in 2020. An enthusiastic researcher and translator, she actively writes, publishes and lectures on diverse contemporary thrust areas like literature and environment, travel and culture, marginalisation and Dalits, memory, recollection and life narratives.